'Jodie's thoughtful, developmentally-informed approach is apparent throughout this book, which provides a comprehensive introduction to ACT with children. Incorporating many helpful examples and child-friendly metaphors, along with chapters dedicated to working with parents and neurodivergent populations, this text will be a great resource for child therapists.'

– Dr Fiona Zandt, clinical psychologist and author of the *Creative Ways to Help Children* series

'Building on a deep appreciation of children as whole humans with valid needs, Jodie shows us how to distil powerful concepts into practical, fun and engaging activities that will capture young people's imagination and allow you to work confidently and playfully with kids of all ages.'

– Jennifer Kemp, author of *The ACT Workbook for Perfectionism* and co-author of *The Neurodivergent Skills Workbook for Autism and ADHD*

'This is an incredibly useful guide for all therapists using ACT with children – both neurotypical and neurodivergent. Covering everything from OCD to ADHD, it translates ACT into simple, fun, jargon-free interventions that kids can easily understand and apply – and also gives invaluable guidance for working with parents. Highly recommended!'

– Russ Harris, author of *ACT Made Simple* and *The Happiness Trap*

'This book peels back the curtain and lets you step into the therapy room of a master child psychologist. Do step in. Once you're in the room (this book) with Jodie, she reveals how to make your work with children engaging and fun while increasing your effectiveness. You will experience what profound acceptance with children looks like. You will discover how to help kids and their families know they are not deficient but, instead, need learning opportunities that fit their individuality. I have no doubt the lessons in this book will be useful for you. It covers everything from how to set up and plan your intervention, to playing games and making them clinically useful. Your sessions will be more fun while also being grounded in good science.'

– Louise Ha⟨ ⟩NA-V founder and bestselling author

D1603593

Acceptance and Commitment Therapy with Children

of related interest

Building Better Therapeutic Relationships with Children
A Creative Activity Workbook
Deborah Schroder
ISBN 978 1 78775 968 8
eISBN 978 1 78775 969 5

Conversation-Starters for Working with Children and Adolescents After Trauma
Simple Cognitive and Arts-Based Activities
Dawn D'Amico, LCSW, PhD
ISBN 978 1 78775 144 6
eISBN 978 1 78775 145 3

Superhero Therapy for Anxiety and Trauma
A Professional Guide with ACT and CBT-based Activities and Worksheets for All Ages
Janina Scarlet
Illustrated by Dean Rankine
Foreword by Dennis Tirch
ISBN 978 1 78775 554 3
eISBN 978 1 78775 555 0

Creative Ways to Help Children Manage Anxiety
Ideas and Activities for Working Therapeutically with Worried Children and Their Families
Dr Fiona Zandt and Dr Suzanne Barrett
Illustrated by Richy K. Chandler
Foreword by Dr Karen Cassiday
ISBN 978 1 78775 094 4
eISBN 978 1 78775 095 1

Acceptance and Commitment Therapy with Children

Applications and Strategies for Anxiety, Depression, Autism, ADHD, OCD and More

JODIE WASSNER

FOREWORD BY **BEN SEDLEY**

Jessica Kingsley Publishers
London and Philadelphia

First published in Great Britain in 2024 by Jessica Kingsley Publishers
An imprint of John Murray Press

1

Copyright © Jodie Wassner 2024

A CIP catalogue record for this title is available from the
British Library and the Library of Congress

ISBN 978 1 83997 582 0
eISBN 978 1 83997 584 4

Printed and bound in Great Britain by TJ Books Limited

Jessica Kingsley Publishers' policy is to use papers that are natural,
renewable and recyclable products and made from wood grown in
sustainable forests. The logging and manufacturing processes are expected
to conform to the environmental regulations of the country of origin.

Jessica Kingsley Publishers
Carmelite House
50 Victoria Embankment
London EC4Y 0DZ

www.jkp.com

John Murray Press
Part of Hodder & Stoughton Ltd
An Hachette Company

Dedicated to all of the children who have entered my therapy room. Thank you for your trust, your humour and your wisdom.

Contents

Foreword

I first met Jodie Wassner at an Acceptance and Commitment Therapy Conference (ANZACBS) in Wellington, New Zealand, in 2015. She was excited to present her newly developed Mindtrain programme, and I was the conference programme chair who unhelpfully put her workshop at the same time as another workshop about working with young people run by one of the ACT community's biggest names. This meant only a small number of us attended Jodie's workshop, which may have been disappointing to Jodie but was a real treat for those of us who were there. At the time, I remember being excited by the possibilities of the programme and was looking forward to seeing it develop even more.

You now hold in your hands a culmination of all of Jodie's hard work, clinical experience and creativity. It is a guide to how to use Acceptance and Commitment Therapy with children and their families. However, it could also be marketed as an introduction to juggling. To work with children, you need to juggle their developmental needs, their cognitive needs, their emotional needs, their needs in each of their contexts – home, school and everywhere else. You also need to juggle the needs of their parents and their school and what everybody's expectations are when they enter the clinical room. In addition, clinicians need to keep in mind what the research says to provide empirically supported treatment and at the same time listen to their clinical instincts and work in a way that is consistent with their own individual personality. That's a lot of balls to keep in the air, and yet Jodie guides the reader through each area so that everything is considered.

More importantly, Jodie's creativity and sense of fun shine through in this book. Over the past few years, Jodie and I have been involved in lots of ACT Follies where conference attendees take ideas from ACT and hold them lightly. On numerous occasions, Jodie has shown how to bring the FUN to FUNctional assessment and this sense of humour is evident in many of the clinical examples and metaphors in this book. She shows that you don't need to be boring and serious to help serious problems; in fact, sometimes the best way to deal with heavy thoughts and feelings is to hold them lightly.

In this book, you will learn practical ways to present each of the Acceptance and Commitment Therapy processes to families without using any jargon or off-putting clinical language. Instead, children will learn about these ideas through fun activities and relatable metaphors. Families will feel validated and ready to make changes at home that will empower their children to respond to their internal experiences and to the external world in more effective ways. You will also learn a number of different metaphors and exercises so that you can try each and then find the ones that work best for you and the families you work with.

Working with children and families is challenging. We want to help them create positive cycles so they can move their own lives in valued directions and we need to do it in ways that aren't judgemental or that underestimate how stressful life can be. I'm sure every reader will take ideas from this book and feel more confident and flexible in their clinical work.

As a clinician who works with young people and their families, and as a parent myself, I thank Jodie for writing this book and every reader for your motivation and commitment to help families thrive.

Ben Sedley
Clinical psychologist, father of three and author of *Stuff that Sucks: A Teen's Guide to Accepting What You Can't Change and Committing to What You Can* and co-author of *Stuff That's Loud: A Teen's Guide to Unspiralling When OCD Gets Noisy* (with Dr Lisa Coyne)

Acknowledgements

I would like to thank the ACT community, my professional family, who inspire me both academically and personally by guiding me in a life direction that has purpose and fulfilment. I'd particularly like to thank Ben Sedley for his wisdom and wit, and for writing a heartfelt foreword for this book.

I would like to gratefully thank Mum and Allan for instilling in me a love of learning and a commitment to hard work, as well as providing me with the early opportunities to pursue my professional dreams. To Dad, whose proudest life achievement was the publishing of his own book. Dad, you always encouraged me to write and provided me with endless confidence in my ability to do the same.

There are many people who helped to shape the content in this book: Thank you to Glenn Fleming, who first motivated me to start writing and sharing the ACT techniques we developed for children, by collaborating to produce Mindtrain. Thank you to the team at Jessica Kingsley Publishing, particularly Jane Evans, for steering this first-timer through the world of publishing. Your faith and guidance have allowed the process to develop seamlessly. Finally, to Ellie Newton, for creating the illustrations and diagrams and for your untiring commitment to the world of books.

To Jane Nethercote: Your wonderful counsel, professionally and personally, are valued more than you can know. Thank you, my magnificent friend.

To my family: Nick, Ellie, Comet and Patsy. I want to gratefully acknowledge your unwavering support over the years. We are so lucky to have one another and I love you all deeply.

Finally, I would like to express my sincerest gratitude to the many children with whom I have worked. It has been a great privilege to hear your stories and witness all of your milestones, struggles and successes as you grow older. It is through interactions with you that the ideas in this book have come to life. When I am in the therapy room, professional boundaries prevent me from expressing how much I admire each of you. I always knew I wanted to work with children and am so glad I followed my heart. Kids are the best.

Jodie

Introduction

I was lucky enough to grow up in a big family. As a teenager, one would often find me playing with my younger cousins, not because I was rejected by the older ones, but because I simply loved hanging out with the little ones. I have always harboured a genuine knack for engaging well with kids. I had a notable instinct for recognizing what children enjoyed and could readily deliver an entertaining afternoon. I was also a bit of a teaching enthusiast and relished my ability to educate my younger cousins about all kinds of things or occasionally encourage them to do something cheeky. I noticed what worked and what didn't work, and I paid particular attention to how different kids learn and how to get them motivated and enthusiastic to play the games I had invented. That was all before I finished high school.

Studying psychology was a wonderful choice for me. During my Honours year, most of my peers applied for a masters in clinical psychology. They weren't surprised to hear that I was applying for a masters in educational and developmental psychology. My professional journey was finally merging with my passion. My first job after registration was as a school psychologist in 1999, where I had the opportunity to work with young people in a typical environment. In 2003 I attended my first Acceptance and Commitment Therapy (ACT) workshop. Very few Australian therapists had heard of ACT at the time and there were only ten of us in a small room in Melbourne, discovering what ACT had to offer. Although the workshop was an introduction to ACT with adults, I was immediately taken with the concepts and embarked on adapting the strategies for the teenagers and children at school. The results were profound. Importantly, I had come to recognize that ACT is not simply about symptom reduction or fixing what is wrong. Rather, ACT promotes a change of outlook that one can carry through life. It is about finding meaning for oneself and behaving in a valued direction despite the inevitable obstacles. It is a willingness to shake off old habits and be flexible enough to reflect on what is truly workable and meaningful. I felt excited and privileged to have the opportunity to teach these skills to young people whose habits and beliefs were still evolving.

Having a young person in a therapy room is a great responsibility. We have the chance to teach and encourage habits of thinking that are workable in the long term. We can help children to pause and think about what is truly important to them and recognize that a valued life is not simply about feeling good all of the time. We don't wait for obstacles to disappear or wish them away. We can help children to find ways to behave in line with their values, even in the presence of obstacles.

The aim of this book is to develop therapists' understanding of ACT and assist them to use it successfully with children. The strategies come from 25 years in the therapy room and are grounded in evidence-based cognitive and behavioural strategies. The approach is accepting, compassionate and affirming.

Many therapists justifiably worry about a child's capacity to truly grasp the inherently abstract concepts that comprise ACT. Working with children is an art; one cannot simply apply strategies without truly considering the individual child. A good child therapist must read where the child is at, not just in terms of their age or intellectual ability, but also in terms of their emotional capacity and environmental context on any given day. True connection with the child is the crucial foundation upon which any therapeutic interaction stands. Only once this is achieved can we start the work of teaching strategies in a child-friendly way.

Over the years, I have had many requests to impart these skills to therapists. This book is much more than an intervention manual. It is a detailed clinical guide to *seeing* children and recognizing how best to engage them while pausing to reflect on one's owns reactions as a therapist and notice how they impact the therapeutic bond. The approach is above all playful. Not only is play fun, but it is a very natural form of communication for children. Therapists often worry that spending too much time in play is wasting time. They might be keen to get stuck into worksheets or cognitive strategies. Play, however, provides children with enormous opportunities for implicit skill building. Children find joy in play, which enables them to feel more relaxed and flexible in the therapy room, so they can be ready for skill development. Play also provides the therapist with an opportunity to role model appropriate language and social skills.

Throughout this book, you will learn child-friendly language to help children notice and respond to their inner experiences such as thoughts and feelings. You will discover visual tools, games, mindfulness exercises, metaphors and toys that will assist children to recognize those patterns of thinking that may be interfering with a valued life. You will also find ways to coach caregivers/parents in these methods so they can assist the young person to unhook from overwhelming thoughts and feelings as they emerge. The skills are applicable to a wide range of presentations including, but not limited to, anxiety, depression and phobias. There are two separate chapters for treating more complex presentations; obsessive compulsive disorder (Chapter 9) and neurodivergence (Chapter 10). Chapter 10 is a neuro-affirming comprehensive approach with a deep focus on autism and attention deficit hyperactivity disorder (ADHD).

There is a separate chapter for working with parents/caregivers (Chapter 11). You will be guided to teach parents about the subtleties in their own language that may be feeding unhelpful beliefs around difficulty. An ACT approach guides parents to resist the instinct to control, fix or stop an unpleasant feeling in their child. Of course, it is painful to watch one's child in distress, but we need to consider the long-term impact of dismissing a child's experience of that distress. Parents will often hide the truth or tell their children that nothing is wrong in an attempt to help their child feel better in that moment. Many parents even tell their children that they have misinterpreted their own emotions or body signals. Signals can sometimes be confusing, so it is important that adults assist a child to notice and interpret their body signals appropriately. We can teach children to notice their internal signals and respond in a way that is workable. In other words, engage in acceptance. By teaching acceptance, we assist children to handle difficulty when it emerges. After all, problems are inevitable. We can assist parents and their children to move away from controlling emotions and towards accepting them. In so doing, we are guiding families towards a valued life that encompasses healthy relationships, strength of character and resilience. We are assisting children to make wise choices based on values rather than avoidance of fear.

As an ACT therapist, I am constantly mindful of the role of language. In the interests of ease, I will be referring to 'parents' throughout the book, although the term is intended to extend to guardians and other caregivers. I am also aware that language changes over time and a term that was deemed appropriate five years ago may no longer be so. One example close to my heart is the term 'autism spectrum disorder (ASD)'. This term is used widely by health practitioners and families alike. Over recent years, I have become increasingly aware of the problematic nature of the term, as it suggests that autism is something that is broken and requires fixing. Neurodiversity describes the idea that people perceive and interact with the world in many different ways. Differences are not viewed as deficits or disorders – hence the preference for the term 'autistic', which I now embrace wholeheartedly. As an ACT therapist, I always try to practice acceptance, compassion and a love of diversity. At the time of writing this book, I believe I am using language that is appropriate to the time and ask for understanding should preferred terms change in the future.

Many case examples are used throughout this book. Some are based on anonymized versions of real cases and others are hypothetical. It is my hope that the examples will be familiar to therapists and can be generalized to the children who enter your rooms. Often when we discover new therapeutic ideas, it can feel exciting but overwhelming as we are unsure about how to start implementing them. We might like the new ideas but fall back into our old repertoires, never using the new tools. The educational and developmental psychologist in me would like to make a small scaffolded suggestion for you. Start off by choosing two strategies from this book and think of suitable children with whom you are willing to have a go. Commit to implementing the two new strategies at least three times over the next few weeks. It might feel awkward initially, so find a way to tweak it to suit your natural style. Over time you will find ways to incorporate more ideas. Be flexible and creative but, most importantly, have fun!

Chapter 1

A Developmental Context

Working with children in a therapeutic context is a privilege like no other. As therapists, we have the opportunity to become part of a young person's life; to guide, to listen and to shape the way they approach the world. Children live within varied contexts that facilitate the development of their views about life. Beliefs, opinions and ideas for approaching the world are readily adopted by young people, especially when picked up from parents, teachers and peers. Some of these beliefs help children to thrive. Others might invite unnecessary struggle.

One belief common to modern western society relates to the narrative suggesting we should be happy most, if not all, of the time. Children learn that it is inappropriate or even naughty to have 'negative' thoughts or feelings. This expands to an assumption that when we have too many unpleasant feelings such as anger, sadness, anxiety or distress, we must be wrong or broken in some way (Harris 2009). An Acceptance and Commitment Therapy (ACT) approach, on the other hand, fosters acceptance of difficulty (Hayes, Strosahl and Wilson 1999). This applies to problematic life events as well as internal difficulties such as anxiety, sadness or troublesome thoughts.

One key feature of an ACT approach is the promotion of psychological flexibility. Psychological flexibility invites us to recognize the problem that accompanies the human tendency to struggle with unpleasant inner experiences such as thoughts and feelings. ACT encourages us to be willing to accept difficulty, despite it being unpleasant, for the purpose of something greater in the long term. We will be inviting young people to behave more effectively based on long-term values rather than engaging in behaviours driven by avoidance of fear. Psychological flexibility promotes the recognition of the benefits that come with moving towards those things in life that truly matter to us, while also noticing and accepting the pain and difficulty that inevitably go with it.

One of the great benefits of working with children is that their belief systems are continually evolving, providing an opportunity to encourage flexibility around these rather complex concepts. Healthier approaches to difficulty can be taught, while unhelpful and rigid beliefs are prevented from becoming deeply entrenched. In a therapeutic context, children can be guided to recognize the value of accepting difficulty, enabling them to spend more time engaging with those things that matter most.

The development of life's simple assumptions

All humans carry assumptions about the way things are or should be. Our history, relationships, beliefs and current circumstances delicately interweave to create how we perceive and, indeed, react in any given situation. Consider the way in which we structure our daily lives. Our cultural rituals, the way we eat, sleep or even wash, are strongly determined by the way we grow up. The subtleties around *how* we speak or carry out these usual tasks are less obvious. It will be these subtleties that powerfully permeate our subconscious and impact our reactions throughout our lifespan.

A simple example relates to pronunciation. Take the letter 'h', which in English is usually pronounced 'aitch', though many say 'haitch'. Your choice of pronunciation is typically determined according to where you grew up and how you first encountered the word. Regardless of what formal diction might rule, many will vehemently insist that the way they first learned to pronounce 'h' is the correct way. This is one simple example of the impact our early learning experiences have on the way we believe things *should* be.

Imagine two university graduates who, after growing up in the same culture and within the same city, decide to move in together after dating for a year. No doubt they have reasonably similar ideas about meals, work, leisure and daily schedules. The intricacies of how households should run may tell a different story. I recall a couple who argued about the clearing of plates after dinner. One believed that each person should carry their own plate to the sink following dinner. The other believed that if one person stood up first, they should take both their own plate and that of their partner. The couple entered into constant arguments, with one expressing, 'I'm not your slave', and the other responding, 'I'm not your housemate'. Each had grown up in households with different assumptions around how plates should be cleared from the table. Beneath the surface of this ongoing argument lie important beliefs, sometimes deeply hurtful, regarding a perceived lack of respect from one another. Understanding the role of these contextual factors can help a therapist determine the function or why of a behaviour.

Childhood assumptions about difficulty

All children grow up in environments filled with assumptions about the way things are supposed to be. From a very young age, we absorb the language and messaging that underpin our culture. This extends to how we make sense of our thoughts, feelings and urges. The modern western narrative around the pursuit of happiness is particularly influential in this way, with media, including social media, reinforcing these beliefs by encouraging the posting of only our happiest images and thoughts. Indeed, posting a comment on social media about feeling personally sad would likely be considered inappropriate or attention-seeking (political comments and recent loss responses excepted).

Parents often exaggerate their children's successes (online and in person) and will hide evidence of any type of failure. In therapy, parents privately report the strain they feel trying to keep up with other families. It is certainly difficult to gain an accurate perspective on how others are doing when we only see one part of reality.

When I ask parents what they want for their children, the usual response is, 'I just want my kids to be happy.' As a parent myself, I understand this sentiment and, of course, very much relish the feeling of seeing my child happy. Placing happiness on a pedestal in this way, however, heightens our efforts to constantly attain it. The deeply ingrained message about the pursuit of happiness unsurprisingly increases our expectations that it is entirely attainable most of the time. However, difficulty and suffering are normal and, in fact, necessary parts of life.

Parent responses to difficulty

Working with children inevitably involves spending time with their parents. Parents, too, may have been brought up in a society that advocates assumptions around the constant pursuit of happiness. Children often take parents' *shoulds* and *musts* as literal truths, so it is especially important to ensure time is spent coaching parents to recognize the impact of their own language, especially in response to hardship.

The language adults use when assisting a young person to approach difficulty holds an important lesson for the developing child's understanding of what to do when experiencing a difficult thought or feeling. A parent's well-intentioned attempts to assist a young person in distress can unknowingly reinforce the message that their feelings are wrong. A sad child in tears may be told, 'Don't cry.' While we appreciate the adult's genuine efforts to make the child feel better, the child may learn that their feelings are incorrect or that they should be able to control their feelings.

Chapter 11 reflects on methods for assisting parents to recognize their responses when they encounter their own adult difficulties. Strategies for assisting parents to manage their own inner struggles within an ACT-consistent framework are provided. This work will be crucial for assisting parents to adjust their language so they are modelling acceptance of difficulty in preparation for their job of coaching their child to do the same.

Common examples of well-intentioned messages from adults to children include:

There's nothing to be scared of.

You could do it last week.

Don't cry.

Thunder can't hurt you.

Don't be ridiculous; there are no sharks in the swimming pool.

Pull it together.

He didn't mean it; you're just too sensitive.

The impact of such messaging is two-fold.

The first problem relates to the dismissive nature of the message. The child feels neither heard nor believed, increasing their anxiety and minimizing their chances of managing the distress effectively.

The second problem pertains to the impact of believing that their feelings are inappropriate. The adult comment implies that the child's feelings are invalid (this is not something to be afraid of; therefore your anxiety is an inappropriate response). We know that receiving such a message rarely helps children to feel better. Rather, it increases their distress because their feelings are real and children are, in that moment, unable to do something they *should* be able to do. They cannot stop the anxiety. An extra layer of distress ensues, which increases their sense of struggle, only serving to amplify, not reduce, the very feeling with which they are battling.

When a child is unable to control their uncomfortable feelings, they may start to believe they are defective in some way. A child who feels broken or abnormal can start to believe that they do not belong, and fear of rejection can follow. The drive to belong is a fundamental human experience. From an evolutionary perspective, our ancient human ancestors who were most successfully able to fit in and cooperate effectively within a group had the best chance of survival and passing on their genes. Those who attempted life without a group or tribe typically had less chance of survival. People today have inherited this strong drive. Children harbour an especially strong need to belong within the family group. Young children certainly do need a family/group for physical survival. Their emotional urge to belong is equally strong. When a young person is told that their unpleasant feelings are wrong, they may experience anxiety regarding the security of their position in the family group. This is particularly powerful if their feelings have resulted in a behaviour that is considered 'naughty'. Unpleasant thoughts often follow:

Does my family like me?

Am I causing too much trouble for my parents?

They never believe me.

Do they even want me here?

The early years are crucial for developing a sense of self as an individual but also in the context of group identity. A child who believes their unpleasant thoughts are abnormal will frequently doubt their capacity to truly belong. In the long term, repeatedly believing that one's thoughts and feelings are inappropriate can lead to lifelong patterns of avoidance.

Avoidance

EXPERIENTIAL ACTIVITY

1. Take a moment to write down some of the unpleasant thoughts or feelings that you, as an adult, sometimes experience.

2. Write down some of the things you might do or say to block out or avoid these inner experiences.

3. Take a moment to write down some of the unpleasant thoughts or feelings that young people sometimes hold.

4. Write down some of the things young people might do or say to block out or avoid these inner experiences.

Common behaviours used by young people to avoid difficult thoughts or feelings may include:

- gaming
- watching YouTube
- refusing to do school work
- eating unhealthy snacks
- procrastination
- running away
- hitting
- yelling
- school avoidance
- refusing social invitations.

For many of these examples, the appeal is obvious. Games are fun, sugar is delicious and television is easier than homework. The appeal is less obvious for some of the other examples, especially when they have such instant negative ramifications, such as the consequences that come from hitting or swearing. The simple answer might be that they have engaged in the behaviour impulsively. A functional explanation might additionally assert that there are secondary benefits to hitting someone, such as the fact that when I hit someone, I get sent out of the room. When a young person is overwhelmed in a busy room, hitting someone might just be their ticket out of that environment.

Avoidance of difficulty is a common human trait at any age. One reason we might avoid is because society tells us that we should be able to control our feelings. If a young person is feeling overwhelmed, the quickest way to regain control is to avoid the very situation that created those feelings. It is easy to see why avoidance is such a tempting solution.

The other perceived benefit of avoidance is that short-term benefits frequently accompany it. When I feel bad, I can avoid what it is that I don't like and feel instant relief. I can feel frustrated by my difficult homework, close my book and watch television instead. Avoiding my homework in this situation has given me a lovely, pleasant feeling as I watch television and don't need to think about mathematics. This strategy is wonderfully effective in the short term. The problem is that my homework still needs to be done. The avoidance has not made the problem go away. In fact, avoiding homework frequently exacerbates the problem because the quantity increases each time I avoid. Furthermore, it will not be long before guilt and hopelessness creep back in. In ACT terms, the avoidance of inner difficulty is referred to as 'experiential avoidance'.

Experiential avoidance

Experiential avoidance refers to human attempts to avoid unpleasant inner sensations, including thoughts, feelings and urges. Children can be taught to recognize the pitfalls of avoiding these unpleasant inner sensations. Before doing so, however, it will be important to ensure they understand the difference between inner and outer experiences.

The terms *outside stuff* and *inside stuff* can be adopted to assist understanding. *Outside stuff* refers to anything we can detect via our five senses. It relates to the things we see, touch, smell, taste or hear. *Inside stuff* refers to anything we notice inside our bodies, such as thoughts, memories or urges. It can also refer to emotions (e.g. angry, excited, frustrated) as well as physical sensations (e.g. hunger, feeling hot, pain, busting for the toilet). Many children struggle with this distinction, but it is an important one to make, and a child's understanding should not be rushed.

A useful strategy for teaching this distinction can be as simple as saying, 'Imagine I had a camera in your house. What would I see you doing?' This suggestion reinforces the concept that outside stuff can be noticed by others looking in. It is often necessary to probe further, as children might provide simple responses such as 'doing nothing' or 'being lazy'. A reminder of the camera and a suggestion that you want to notice what their body is actually doing can sometimes assist with the recognition of what is going on via their five senses.

Therapist: Yes, but when you are being lazy, where might you be sitting? Would you be holding anything? Looking at something?

GAME: INSIDE VERSUS OUTSIDE

Some children will enjoy a quick game to reinforce their understanding of the difference between outer and inner experiences. The therapist creates a stack of cards, with each card describing either an outer experience or an inner experience. The therapist and child take turns drawing cards from the pack and placing them either on the outer pile or the inner pile. Each is timed to see who can tell the difference the fastest.

Card examples

Outer experience	Inner experience
Smelling dinner	Thirsty
Seeing my friend	Worry
Tasting chocolate	Itchy
Hearing the bell	Thinking about my party
Patting my dog	Having the thought 'This is hard'
Unpacking my school bag	Remembering last Christmas
Opening the door	Headache

Avoidance of inner difficulty

Once the child has mastered the art of noticing the difference between inner and outer experiences, we can begin to recognize the problems associated with avoiding unpleasant inner sensations.

Imagine a shy child who is reluctant to approach other children due to a fear (inner experience) of being rejected. The child can easily move away from this uncomfortable fear. They can choose to sit alone every lunchtime and decline party invitations. This would ensure that they are never rejected and can never feel the hurt that accompanies rejection.

> I do not like the feeling of rejection, so I move away from any situation where it could potentially appear.

Over time, the withdrawal from other people and the ability to avoid feeling rejected are reinforced. The child feels relief each time they move away from a potentially anxiety-provoking social interaction. By never connecting with others and withdrawing further from society, that child's world becomes smaller and smaller, with less opportunity and less meaning.

I once worked with a young boy who had an extreme fear of wind. He was unable to tolerate the slightest movement of a tree in the wind for fear it would become a disastrous tornado. Over time, the boy's world became smaller; he spent playtime at the school's front office instead of playing with his friends. He passed most of his time at home in a dark study with the curtains closed. Eventually, he was barely able to leave his house. As it is a well-known film, I chose to use *The Wizard of Oz* (1939) to create a metaphor that would help the child recognize the cost of his slow withdrawal from the world.

METAPHOR: *THE WIZARD OF OZ*

Therapist: Can you remember that scene in *The Wizard of Oz* when the tornado arrives in Kansas? Aunty Em, Uncle Henry and all of the farm helpers run into an underground bunker. They lift the hatch, scramble downstairs, close the hatch and wait for the tornado to pass.

Why do you think they did that?

That's right, they are safe underground. The tornado can't hurt them there. Once the tornado passes, they can open the hatch and come back out safely. It seems like that underground bunker was a great idea, and it kept them all safe.

What do you think it looked like inside that bunker?

Probably just soil, maybe bits of wood. I wonder if they were organized enough to have any supplies down there. Perhaps there were some food tins or water bottles. Maybe not. I guess it was pretty dirty, dark, and boring down there.

So, remind me, why did they go down there?

That's right; it kept them safe.

Now I'd like you to imagine that a week later, there's just a little bit of wind over the farm. Should they go down there again?

Depends? Okay, so what would happen if they went down every single time there was a little bit of wind? How often do you think they would go down there? Probably every day. Shouldn't they do that? After all, wouldn't that keep them safe? What's the problem with running down there every time there is a little bit of wind?

And what kind of life would that be? It doesn't sound like a very interesting life to me.

If they want to have a truly fulfilling life, it sounds like they need to be outside of that bunker, enjoying farm life. But to do this, they need to tolerate a little bit of uncertainty about the weather. They need to find a way to handle a little bit of worry each time there is wind.

This metaphor, although originally designed for wind phobia, can be applied to many situations to illustrate the problem with avoidance.

Acceptance of difficulty

Acceptance is the antithesis of avoidance and is a key element of an ACT approach. Acceptance within an ACT framework refers to a willingness to experience difficult thoughts and feelings, including unwanted ones such as fear, and then choose to behave effectively and flexibly based on values. Acceptance is not a resignation to the fact that life will be difficult. We do not need to like the difficulty. We are encouraged to notice the difficulty, carry that difficulty with us, and still move forward in a meaningful direction.

QUICKSAND METAPHOR

The quicksand metaphor is a well-known technique within ACT (Hayes *et al.* 1999), highlighting the problem that comes from avoiding or struggling with difficulty. Children's cartoons deserve credit for the fact that many young people are familiar with the concept of a cowboy falling into quicksand. A picture or some decent acting can help with effective delivery.

Therapist: Have you ever seen quicksand? Do you know what you are supposed to do if you fall into quicksand? What happens if you do this?

(Therapist flaps arms and mimics treading water with a struggle.)

That's right, you sink more and more quickly. So, the trick with quicksand is to try to stay still. The more we struggle, the more we sink.

The same goes for troublesome feelings such as worry. If worry shows up and we start to struggle or hate the worry, it just grows bigger and bigger.

DEVIL'S SNARE METAPHOR

Referencing a child's interests can be an extremely effective way to illustrate concepts. Therapists should familiarize themselves with child-friendly popular culture and trends to ensure explanations are relevant. For Harry Potter fans, the concept of *Devil's Snare* (*Harry Potter and the Philosopher's Stone* 2001) is a great way to illustrate the troubles that accompany a struggle with difficulty. During the film, three characters, Harry, Ron and Hermione, find themselves strangled by a plant with snake-like tendrils. The more they struggle, the more the plant strangles their bodies. Hermione suggests they relax and, sure enough, she becomes able to slide out of the grips of the plant.

These metaphors are simple and fun ways to demonstrate that struggling can amplify difficulty. While metaphors can be used to explain a concept, real-life examples are an essential part of child psychoeducation.

The following technique can be applied to many real-life examples to further describe the problem that accompanies the struggle with difficulty. It should be acknowledged that the exercise includes the terms 'clean bother' and 'dirty bother' to describe uncomfortable sensations. ACT, in its purest form, encourages us to observe sensations without judgement, and the terms 'clean' and 'dirty' may be interpreted as good and bad. I have attempted this technique with terms that are less evaluative but have noticed poorer outcomes in the child's learning and the utility of the technique. In the interest of workability, I have decided to proceed with the terms 'clean' and 'dirty'. Should you wish to try terms that are less evaluative, colours such as 'purple bother' and 'grey bother' are suggested.

DIRTY BOTHER – CLEAN BOTHER

Therapist: I'm going to draw two circles like this. We are going to name the inner circle 'Clean Bother' and the outer bit here 'Dirty Bother'.

(Younger children may require the therapist to clarify 'bother', e.g. feeling upset, worried or angry inside.)

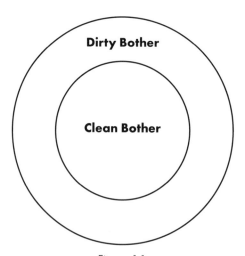

Figure 1.1

Now let's imagine that everybody in your grade is required to present a speech to the whole class. Today is the day, and all the children are sitting at their desks with their speeches ready in their hands. They are all waiting to see which student will be chosen first. Do you think most kids would be nervous?

I do. I think most kids will be a bit nervous, and they might notice their tummy feels weird or their heart races a bit.

(The therapist proceeds to write physiological sensations inside the inner circle.)

They might be thinking things like...

Will the teacher think my speech is good?

Have I prepared the right thing?

Will the kids like my speech?

Will I stay within the time limit?

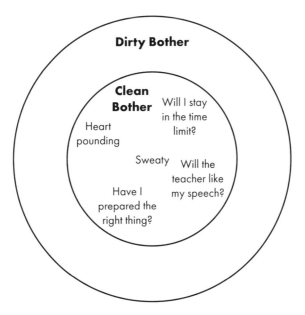

Figure 1.2

Most people worry before giving speeches, and these are the sorts of thoughts and feelings most people would have. It's not comfortable, but most of us can have these feelings and still deliver a good speech.

There are some kids who get *extra* stressed when they notice these uncomfortable thoughts and feelings. They start to worry that the feelings mean something is very wrong. When that happens, this inside bother (pointing to the inner circle) doesn't stop there. It becomes like a magnet and starts to attract bigger feelings and thoughts (start pointing towards the outer circle).

The therapist writes in the outer circle.

Figure 1.3

Oh no, my heart is racing; there must be something wrong with me.

Why are my legs shaking? What if the kids notice? I'll be so embarrassed.

What if my voice gets shaky and I say the wrong words?

The therapist can refer to the outer circle (Dirty Bother) and explain that it is this extra layer of struggle that causes the bigger problem. The feeling of Clean Bother represents a typical level of discomfort that can show up in any situation. For most people, we can feel it and still get on with our task. By struggling with or attaching meaning to this initial bother, as seen in the outer circle, we are inviting an unnecessary layer of extra difficulty. It is this extra layer of difficulty (Dirty Bother) that is often responsible for much higher levels of distress and poorer coping. Unfortunately, once this has happened, it is more likely that the child will indeed make errors or fumble through their speech, reinforcing their belief that they cannot do it.

Cognitive techniques will be covered in Chapter 8 to demonstrate how an acceptance approach to that initial difficulty (Clean Bother) enables a more manageable outcome.

The following chapters will delve into strategies for enabling young people to notice difficulty, accept difficulty and choose to move in a valued direction. We will discuss ideas for identifying a valued life and motivating a willingness to engage in the hard stuff kids need to do to move towards it.

Summary

Upbringing plays a key role in framing the beliefs we hold that influence the way we approach difficulty. ACT acknowledges that difficulty and suffering are normal and expected parts of life. When they show up, we work towards accepting the difficulty rather than avoiding or struggling with it. By reducing the struggle, we are reframing the potential power of that difficulty. It is important to recall that we are not trying to rid ourselves of the problem entirely, for we know this only increases the struggle. Language is crucial; it can be tempting to say that a strategy will help you feel less anxious, but this would pull us back into the struggle trap. Rather, we will use language suggesting that when difficulty shows up, we can engage in acceptance-based strategies that move us towards the life we truly want to live. These skills are best learnt in a context in which the child feels safe and heard, highlighting the importance of a compassionate, flexible and accepting approach within the therapy room.

• Chapter 2 •

Connecting Authentically with Children

When young people arrive at their first therapy session, they carry varying expectations. Some arrive excitedly, ready to be helped. Many are forced into our rooms following poor experiences with other practitioners. Others arrive unsure of how things might work and what to expect. One thing they all have in common, however, is a need to feel heard and believed. Acceptance and Commitment Therapy (ACT) provides therapists with an opportunity to create a superb canvas on which to guide interactions with children.

An ACT-friendly environment emphasizes acceptance, compassion and playfulness through a therapist's language and behaviour. ACT in the therapy room requires far more than imparting our knowledge of various tricks and strategies. By prioritizing a sense of compassion in a young person's presence, a child can feel safe, heard and believed, regardless of the presenting issue. Once established, we can begin to direct them towards a valued life via the skills and strategies that are eagerly waiting to emerge from our ACT toolbox.

A canvas of compassion

Compassion-focused therapy (CFT) developed by Professor Paul Gilbert OBE (2009), explores ideas of safety, compassion and reassurance in individuals. Compassion-focused ACT (Tirch, Schoendorff and Silberstein 2014) extends CFT, placing compassion as an active variable within the ACT therapy room. Traditionally, the focus of CFT has been on adults who might have grown up in critical, abusive or neglectful environments. It can be argued that the benefits of CFT may stretch well beyond these types of presentations. Many parents and carers who bring their children to therapy face significant struggle and difficulty, despite their best efforts to provide high levels of intentional care and nurturing to their children. These children may be brought into therapy carrying the self-perspective of 'difficult' child. A child's interaction with a compassion-focused therapist could be the first time they have experienced unconditional acceptance. This, in turn, lowers the threat response and activates the soothing system to establish a sense of safety and trust (Tirch *et al.* 2014). A compassionate environment within therapy can make a significant difference to the child's capacity to remain engaged and benefit from therapy. We cannot teach life skills unless the child believes we are on their team. Once the child feels safe, we can start thinking about more explicit skill building during future sessions.

I often recall a story of a grandparent who once approached me in public, saying, 'I believe you are seeing my grandson.' This can be an awkward moment for any therapist, but I chose to smile and simply say, 'He is so delightful.' I will never forget the look on the grandmother's face as I realized that nobody had ever described her grandson in this way. He had a long history of problems, often getting into trouble at school, and his parents were struggling with his behaviour on a daily basis. My comment, however, was honest and from the heart and had been genuinely reflected in my compassion-focused interactions with him. It is humbling as a therapist to experience these moments, as they shed enormous light on our responsibility to the young people who come into our care. His sense of safety within therapy will prove to be an invaluable asset when we approach the really tough work of emotion regulation in future sessions. When used skilfully, a compassion focus opens up immense possibilities for teaching young people the skills we wish for them to acquire.

Creating a physical environment that supports therapy

Practitioner training and practice standards provide exceptional guidance regarding a therapist's obligations around informed consent. Most therapists do this well, having a well-rehearsed spiel they impart during the first session outlining session processes as well as issues around consent and confidentiality. This sets up expectations around how therapy will proceed. While this is obviously necessary, much of this information is less important to a child than are other contextual features of the room. Setting up the expectations of therapy in a way that is relevant to young people can have a very meaningful impact on the success of therapy.

Imagine a young person entering a room for the first time, feeling uncertain about why they are there, and knowing they will be left alone in this room with an adult they have never met. We need to think carefully about creating a physical setup that will feel most comfortable. The classic couch in a therapy room is rarely appropriate. It screams of 'grown-up' and of a requirement to sit still. It is also extremely uncomfortable if you are too small for your feet to reach the floor. Traditional counselling education teaches therapists to sit still with an open posture, leaning forward with good eye contact. The goal here is to help the patient feel completely heard. These non-verbal cues, however, can be intimidating for children. By allowing children to move around the room, we are minimizing the pressure of intense, uncomfortable engagement.

A welcoming room should offer multiple options for sitting or, if preferred, moving around. These can be tweaked according to intake information. An older child whose referral information suggests low mood and motivation might be best placed in a comfortable chair, much as we might conduct therapy with someone older. A referral of a child with an attention deficit or tendency to fidget, however, would struggle in this setting. They would benefit from being able to move around on various surfaces. When a young person walks into a room and sees multiple options on offer, it can have an immediate impact on their capacity to enter with confidence and feel safe. A therapist seated on a floor rug speaks volumes. There are many wonderful seating options that provide sensory feedback, such as exercise-fit ball seats, bean bags and seat pads. A therapist who can mirror the child's choice of seating will reinforce acceptance and readiness to engage. This does not mean sitting exactly the same way as the child. A therapist can playfully move towards the child's seating choice. For example, I might choose to walk or roll on my wheeled desk chair towards a child seated on an ottoman. This is not only about establishing appropriate physical distance but also creating an atmosphere of lightness. It gives the message that this is not a strict learning space with adult rules. It's a place where I can move as I please and laugh as I please. Children in my room quickly learn that they can sit in any position. Often, they sit upside down for the whole session. I want children to understand that they can sit however they need to in order to feel at ease when they are with me. My goal is for them to be completely relaxed so they can learn.

Enabling a relaxed tone through acceptance

In order to project 'acceptance', a child-friendly demeanour must be adopted by the therapist. This may include adopting casual language, laughing at incidental moments and perhaps even fidgeting a little yourself. A good therapist will be familiar with typical communication interactions at various developmental stages and be able to match those to the child. For example, people automatically use a slower pace of speech and more high-pitched tones when speaking to a pre-schooler. If, however, these methods are used with an older child, they might feel as though they are being treated like a baby. Pitching the pace, rhythm and activities at the right level is extremely important.

Rules around what can be touched and not touched should be established early and framed positively. 'You are welcome to play with any of these fidget toys on the desk'; 'You can touch anything you like on the red shelves.' Items that should not be touched should preferably be kept out of reach, as we do not want to set up a situation in which a child feels they are in trouble in the early stages of therapy.

Even for those children who are able to sit still on a chair, speaking openly with an adult can feel intimidating. It can be useful to use games, diagrams and whiteboards to reduce the pressure to communicate. Sitting at a desk and scribbling down ideas can reduce the pressure for eye contact during discussion. We can focus on the paper or the whiteboard. For older children, we can engage in a combination of games and discussion. Therapists often find they acquire more discussion from a child while shuffling a pack of cards or doing a puzzle than in a straight face-to-face discussion. In order to gain a better flow of conversation with a child, it is often suitable to allow the child to engage in a physical activity during the conversation. Examples include:

- ripping up paper
- bracelet making
- finger knitting

- fidget toys.

It should be noted that when a child is expected to be engaged and attending, fidgeting can sometimes pull their focus away. It is usually very easy to tell whether the child is engaged or disengaged with a therapist while fidgeting. Explaining this to parents will often be necessary. Many parents worry that a child doing something else with their hands will distract them from attending therapy. Children, however, can handle multiple forms of stimulation. In fact, if the therapist has determined that fidgeting has enhanced relaxation, the patient will be more ready for skill development. For many neurodivergent young people, fidgeting will actually enhance their ability to focus on a discussion.

Once we have moved to the skill-building stage of therapy, we will incorporate discussions around the fact that there is a time and a place for sitting still and making eye contact. While it is not always an expectation in the therapy room, it is critical to ensure that children can learn when these skills must be delivered appropriately.

Meeting children where they're at

When a therapist asks a young person about the things they like to do, one often sees a glint in the child's eye. A therapist's level of interest via verbal and non-verbal cues will usually determine the extent to which that child will continue to engage. Most children will have a screen-related topic among their top favourite activities. Children know, though, that adults are constantly telling them about the dangers of screen time. Screens are certainly an issue that can be discussed separately with parents. In the early stages of therapy, a hearty and enjoyable discussion around a child's favourite online game, YouTube channel or television show can build rapport via acceptance at exceptional rates. Early-career therapists often express guilt about spending a session chatting about Minecraft or playing games. Therapy, however, cannot be rushed. Spending time on the child's interests can be an investment in their capacity to skill-build in future sessions.

The best achievement after session one is to send the child home feeling heard and wanting to come back. In some circumstances therapists may have also successfully instilled hope that things can get better.

The language of acceptance

If a therapist makes a clinical judgement that a child is able to engage in conversation about difficulty, it creates an opportunity to model acceptance-based language that focuses on normalizing difficulty. There are two key features of language worth clarifying in the context of acceptance.

Acceptance of inner difficulty

The traditional ACT definition of acceptance emphasizes acceptance of inner difficulties such as thoughts, feelings, urges, beliefs and memories. When humans experience these, their instinct is to try to get rid of the discomfort. ACT theory suggests that it is the struggle with painful thoughts and sensations (avoidance) that can create overwhelming levels of difficulty. These tools will be crucial in helping children reduce their struggles but should be reserved for later stages of therapy due to their complex cognitive load. During earlier stages of therapy, messages around acceptance of inner difficulty may be gently introduced via incidental language around noticing difficulty (e.g. 'That must have been upsetting'; 'I can see why that annoyed you so much').

Unconditional and compassion-focused acceptance

The second type of acceptance refers to a therapist's ability to communicate unconditional acceptance of a young person as they are. This technique is highly compatible with a compassion-focused approach. In Chapter 1, we briefly explored the evolutionary perspective of the human struggle around fear of negative evaluation. Our human ancestors, who lived predominantly in groups, had a far better chance of survival than those who attempted life alone. Accordingly, humans today have inherited a strong drive to cooperate, to fit into the group and to feel as though they belong. When we experience a situation that threatens our sense of belonging, this deep-seated drive can translate into a threat-related behavioural response (fight or flight). When intense and heightened threat responses are frequently activated, they can lead to the emotional and behavioural struggles that bring many young people to the therapy room. Therefore, feeling as though they belong in the family is extremely important for children. A child's ability to feel included, liked and accepted within the family impacts mental health and behaviour. A child who often finds themselves in trouble for their behaviour may question their ability to belong in the family and experience unpleasant thoughts such as:

I'm the difficult child.

I'm not good enough.

I'm too much trouble for my family.

This can enhance the fear of rejection within the family, which may then be compounded as they arrive into the room of a therapist whose job is to 'fix them'. A child who feels accepted and even liked in the therapy room will have better readiness to engage and benefit from any skill development on offer.

Why am I different?

Regardless of the presenting issue, children who come to therapy all want to be helped in some way, whether this is accepted or denied on the surface. Most young people arrive at therapy believing they are the only ones experiencing their specific problem. This can be accompanied by that dreaded sense that they are different, broken or unable to fit in. Some of the unpleasant thoughts that consume young minds as they enter therapy may include:

There's something wrong with me.

I'm the only one who...has a mother like this, still pees her pants, can't handle a sleepover, etc.

Nobody can know about my brother; it's too embarrassing...

I'm the most anxious person in the world.

The undertone of these thoughts suggests a greater struggle that may translate into 'I must keep this secret', 'Nobody can know' or 'I can't control myself'. At an even deeper level, we return to the threat of rejection from the group and the impact on our survival instinct. Higher levels of shame, guilt and secrecy often follow, compounding the struggle and creating an even deeper layer of emotional difficulty. From an ACT perspective, it is this extra layer of struggle that can cause real emotional harm.

In those early stages, the ACT-focused language and behaviour of a therapist can become a subtle but powerful navigator towards reducing struggle. During the initial session, the child needs to feel heard and understood. The therapist's goal is for the child to know that, no matter what their presenting issue is, no matter what incident their parent has described, the therapist is on their team and will back them when necessary.

Acceptance language for externalizing behavioural problems

Acceptance language requires a therapist to impart the sense that they will do their best to understand the child's perspective and will listen to their version of events. Initially, some parents fear that this response is overly permissive and gives the young person approval to continue engaging in inappropriate behaviour. It is important to explain to parents that while the child does need to be held accountable for certain behaviours, that is not the goal in the early stages of therapy. Modelling appropriate language for the child and parent will be crucial at this stage.

Case example: The child's point of view as the gateway to true learning

Charlie, who is 7 years old, was sent home from school for kicking Jack. Multiple adults (parents and teachers) have already held discussions with Charlie covering the following:

Kicking is forbidden.

Jack's feelings are hurt.

What could Charlie do differently next time?

Charlie might arrive at therapy knowing that his new therapist has also heard about the dreaded kicking incident and brace himself for another lecture, this time by another adult, about why kicking is inappropriate. The goal, however, of an ACT-friendly therapist is to reduce anxiety to enable learning. In Chapter 4, we will discuss the neurobiology behind anxiety to explain why learning can rarely occur effectively when the child is stuck in the cycle of blame and excuses.

Instead, we put into action the canvas of acceptance by using language that implicitly indicates that you, as a therapist, are in no way overwhelmed by the child's behaviour and have compassion for the situation he finds himself in. It does not matter what the child has done or why the child has arrived at therapy. You have room to hold whatever has brought him here. A compassionate stance can be established via the therapist's tone, body language and verbal language.

We need to ask ourselves: What is it that Charlie needs right now, and what can be learned? There is a strong probability that Charlie already knows that kicking is inappropriate and that it hurts others. This is therefore not a teaching priority at this moment.

Kicking Jack was most likely an impulsive reaction based on Charlie's frustration. A more workable ACT-focused goal would be to assist Charlie in recognizing when his frustration is growing and enable him to acquire help before he loses control. Charlie, however, is not ready to learn this skill. We know this because Charlie's comments have repeatedly indicated that he remains focused on Jack's actions. To further complicate matters, Charlie feels as though everybody has taken Jack's side.

First, we can help Charlie feel heard and believed.

Therapist: I can see why you kicked Jack. It sounds like he had been annoying you all day. You must have been so frustrated.

This would be a wonderful opportunity to allow Charlie to tell his side of the story. Charlie could relay all the frustrating things Jack had been doing and finally feel as though someone was listening to his side of the story. Charlie's anxiety decreases as he feels heard.

This brings us to a therapeutic crossroads requiring keen clinical judgement. If Charlie is still very worked up about Jack, it may be worth leaving the discussion there and sending him home with the sense that there is an adult who has heard and understands his frustration with Jack. If, however, it seems as though Charlie has relaxed sufficiently and is able to think more clearly, we may be able to take the learning to the next level.

Therapist: So, Jack has been teasing you for weeks, and you're the one who ended up in trouble. How did that happen?

From here we can subtly assist Charlie in recognizing his unworkable behavioural response (kicking). Again, clinical judgement is made as to whether to pursue further reflection or leave matters as they are. If Charlie continues to feel believed and appears open to learning, his perceptual filter is broadened, and he may be able to consider alternative points of view. We can then assist Charlie in problem solving the next time. This would involve noticing frustration increasing, committing to more workable behaviour and accessing help (see Chapter 7).

By accepting Charlie as he is, acknowledging the origin of his behaviour as coming from a place of genuine difficulty, and showing compassion for his situation, Charlie can unhook from blaming and making excuses. Stephen Porges (2009) describes the human brain as a sophisticated system that is constantly assessing whether it is safe or in danger. If it detects safety, then the 'social engagement system' can be activated. When this occurs, the muscles relax, the perceptual filter is broadened and we are able to notice more in the environment. By seeing more, hearing more and noticing more, we become more psychologically flexible and can consider other points of view. Reactive and impulsive responses are simultaneously minimized. When a compassionate approach is effectively delivered to a child such as Charlie, he feels safe enough to shift his focus towards noticing his actions and reflecting on what really went wrong. This is where the true learning happens.

Acceptance language for internalizing behavioural problems

Children who present with internalizing behaviour (withdrawn, quiet) can often have their difficulties dismissed or unnoticed for much longer than a child such as Charlie. They may be experiencing worsening anxiety and mood difficulties and feel as though they are broken, not good enough or a burden to their family. These children may have been told, 'You're too sensitive' or 'That's nothing to cry over.' Language like this can feel rejecting and induce a primal state of threat, limiting the child's available repertoire of behavioural responses.

Modelling acceptance and normalizing anxiety and sensitivity early on contributes significantly to the trajectory of therapy.

Therapist: You would be amazed at how many kids in Grade 5 have never managed a sleepover.

I really love the way you look after your brother. It seems like life is pretty tough for him. He's so lucky to have a brother like you. But I bet there are times when it's really hard for you. Do your friends know about his disability?

Acceptance language for diverse presentations

For children who present as quirky or somewhat different from typical kids, the fear of rejection or not belonging inevitably appears more frequently. For these children, it will be important to explore their quirks and strengths early on, so the therapist can quickly value their difference and enhance their ability to feel accepted. Language that prioritizes acceptance is also a skill that can be taught to parents.

Let us look at the example of a 9-year-old girl whose parents recently received a report suggesting she is on the autism spectrum. The parents could be experiencing mixed emotions and may have questions about when and how to disclose the diagnosis. An acceptance framework recognizes that we celebrate difference and value the uniqueness and strengths of autism. It posits that when we deny or suppress, greater struggles ensue. Of course, disclosing a diagnosis needs to be handled sensitively, and families can present with varying levels of acceptance and readiness. Regardless of where the families are, the child may be feeling confused and craving acceptance.

In order for the young person to feel as though their parents value difference, parents can prepare by creating discussions at home that emphasize acceptance of different types of people. Parents can achieve this incidentally through the subtleties of language. For example, imagine that a mother and daughter are walking down the street when a woman with bright pink hair walks past. The mother could say, 'How ridiculous is that pink hair?' or 'What an individual!' The latter comment provides an implicit message around acceptance or even admiration for difference. Discussions with parents about valuing difference can assist them in demonstrating to their children that they truly admire and accept difference. Parents could be encouraged to consider their own language choices when discussing people from diverse backgrounds.

How do parents talk about immigrants? LGBTQIA+? People with disabilities? Those with unusual tastes?

When parents and therapists use implicit language that suggests a love of difference, they are in a better position to present an autism diagnosis using a strengths approach. Instead of being afraid of difference, this sets them on a path of exploring and valuing the uniqueness of autism. This, in turn, can impact the young person's self-concept and their capacity to navigate their challenges from an easier platform. In comparison, a parent with rigid rules and beliefs about how we should behave and think would experience significantly more difficulty convincing their quirky daughter that they 'like' their differences.

Although the example here relates to the autism spectrum, many kids feel different in many ways, and the concept is certainly applicable more broadly. Therapists who value difference and model a love of diversity to both parents and children via language can expect a young person who is less threatened and more ready to learn.

Getting the language right

Early-career practitioners often raise concerns about the pressure they feel to 'get the language right'. Rigid language scripts can often do more harm than good by preparing the practitioner for a less relaxed approach to the session and influencing the overall mood of the session. Flexibility in language is equally important, and it is not advisable for therapists to enter the room self-consciously with rigid rules around ACT-appropriate language. Many practitioners find that incorporating ACT values and language into their own day-to-day lives eventually leads to a more natural transition into the therapy room.

Using game play as a therapeutic tool

Some of the children who come to therapy have minimal capacity to engage in discussion about difficulties. Carefully chosen game-playing can be a beneficial way to spend time. Many practitioners, particularly those in private practice, are concerned about spending the sessions playing games because they are worried about parents complaining about the cost. These interactions, however, provide far more than a simple game of cards.

The primary benefit of game-playing is the value of a child being in a room with a responsible adult, modelling appropriate interactions through the language of compassion and acceptance, and how we approach difficulty. These benefits cannot be overestimated, particularly in the earlier stages of therapy. The implicit learning that can take place in these circumstances is often more beneficial than explicit skill teaching, such as with psychoeducational worksheets.

The second benefit relates to the implicit teaching of social skills. Many of the children who come to therapy have a theoretical understanding of how we play games. They are generally aware of the importance of taking turns, being a good sport and playing fairly. When a child, however, feels threatened, their capacity to translate this theoretical knowledge into practice can be compromised, leading to conflict with friends. Children who struggle to lose games and take turns are typically lacking in flexibility.

A child playing a game rigidly with an adult therapist would proceed more easily and with less conflict than with a peer. Having set up the therapy room within a canvas of acceptance and compassion, a child may be more likely to engage in appropriate game play. When difficulties arise (e.g. the child notices they are starting to lose the game), the therapist's response can guide the child into more managed rather than reactive responses. These skills need to be practised repeatedly and successfully in order for the child to gain the flexibility required to transfer them to the playground. The therapy room can be viewed as a training space for these skills.

Initially, it can be useful to acknowledge that we sometimes have different rules than our friends, and an important skill for children to learn is how to establish which rules will be played before commencing any game.

Below is an example of an interaction to guide this process during a game of UNO that encourages flexibility. UNO is an excellent choice for teaching this skill because most children are familiar with it and because the rules vary greatly between children. If you are a UNO player, the following will make sense to you. If not, it would be useful to learn the game to enable generalization of the below technique to other games.

EXAMPLE: PLAYING UNO

Therapist: Different families often have different rules in UNO. Let's figure out what rules we'll be using today. Does your family play the Pick Up Put Down rule? Can you stack +2s? What happens if you forget to say UNO?

Ask the child to clarify which of the above rules they usually follow.

Therapist response: Oh, no! My family plays by different rules than your family. What should we do?

This allows for the development of a relaxed and safe environment to negotiate. Depending on the child's flexibility and comfort in the room, the therapist can make a decision about how much to compromise. We can also use the space to negotiate who goes first and who chooses the game we play.

Handling poor game skills in session

When a child presents with poor skills in game playing, a therapist's incidental chatter during a game usually leads to greater learning than a social skills worksheet. For example, if a child begins to move pieces in a board game so that the game can't be continued properly, a therapist might be tempted to say, 'Don't do that. Put the piece back.' Alternatively, an ACT approach would encourage the young person to look at the workability of their behaviour. A therapist expressing, 'That's really annoying, Zac,' may be enough for the child to return the piece. If the behaviour continues, the therapist could say, 'I'm getting bored now; I'm going to do something else.' Withdrawing attention from the inappropriate behaviour enables the young person to reflect on the fact that spoiling the game was not effective.

When playing with a child who has had an unlucky run of cards in a game and is starting to lose, a therapist might notice frustration building. This is a crucial point at which a therapist needs to decide what lesson is most valuable. If it is decided that persistence and being a good loser are the priorities, we might persist with the game but risk the child's frustration overwhelming them, impacting their ability to continue engaging in the session in a meaningful way. Alternatively, we might choose to engage in some subtle acceptance language that enables the child to feel heard.

Therapist: Wow, you've had a really unlucky run. That must be so annoying for you.

By feeling heard and understood and knowing that being in a losing position is a matter of bad luck and not a character deficit, the child may feel in a safer position to lose gracefully.

A therapist might additionally need to make a decision about how to respond when a young person cheats in a game. While cheating is unacceptable, a workability model would suggest that it is only occasionally best to draw attention to it. A child who is dysregulated and unable to handle losing would feel further threatened when challenged about cheating. This takes away from our primary goal of learning. On this occasion, a different lesson, such as turn taking, might be more appropriate. Lessons around cheating may need to wait. A canvas of acceptance and compassion will typically speed up this process.

Within several sessions, therapists find that children will themselves initiate negotiations through games and turn taking. Having achieved and practised these skills successfully in sessions, the child has a greater chance of transferring the flexible play skills to interactions with peers.

Summary

Children are brought to therapy due to a wide range of difficulties. Regardless of whether they acknowledge their role in the difficulties, a canvas of compassion, together with the language of acceptance and understanding, can instil hope that things can get better, as early as the first session. Using ACT goes beyond worksheets, tricks and scripts. Acceptance and compassion can be built in at multiple levels to allow authentic connections with children, via:

- providing a space that provides opportunities to feel safe through movement, play and seating choices

- non-verbal therapist behaviour, such as how they move around the room and respond flexibly to events

- ACT-focused language; compassionate acceptance of difference and of difficulty.

By prioritizing a sense of compassion and acceptance in the early stages of therapy, a child can feel safe, heard and believed. Only once this is established can we begin to direct them towards a valued life through the more complex skills and techniques of ACT.

• Chapter 3 •

Sample First Session

Having established a welcoming setting, as described in Chapter 2, a young person may or may not be ready to enter into discussion about why they have come to therapy.

The following three-part procedure is a technique that can be adapted to most ages during the first session. It allows therapists to pace their questions by providing minimal pressure for the child to discuss emotionally charged topics, but it also provides an opportunity for gathering important information for those young people with a willingness to chat more openly. It includes moving about the room and allowing the child to write on the whiteboard, which most find enjoyable.

Part 1: The problems list

Therapist: Has anybody told you who I am or why you're here? Did you chat about it on the way here?

Child: Not really. Maybe because of school stuff? I don't know.

Therapist: That's okay. Come over to the whiteboard. I'm going to write down a bunch of reasons why kids your age come to see me. You don't have to tell me yes or no just yet. I'll just write the list, and when I'm finished, you can use this whiteboard marker to tick the ones that you think might be true for you.

The therapist moves towards the whiteboard and briefly explains each point on the list, writing them on the whiteboard, one at a time (see Figure 3.1 for completed list).

Therapist: Some kids come to me because they have trouble

concentrating. Don't tell me yet, but if that one is true for you, you'll be able to check it off soon. (Therapist writes 'concentration' on the whiteboard.)

Some kids come to me because they find their school work too hard and seem to need more help than everyone else. They tell me it can get embarrassing for them. (Therapist writes 'school work too hard' on the whiteboard.)

Some kids come because they get into a lot of arguments. It can be with friends or with family. (Therapist writes 'arguments with family' and 'arguments with friends' on the whiteboard.)

A lot of kids have trouble making friends or even keeping friends. (Therapist writes 'making friends' on the whiteboard.)

Many kids come to me because they are having trouble sleeping. Maybe they can't fall asleep until really late. Others wake up in the middle of the night. A lot of the kids tell me that they end up needing their parents for sleep and wish they could do it alone. (Therapist writes 'sleep' on the whiteboard).

Now the next one I'm writing down is a funny one. I'm going to write 'worries' here. (Therapist writes 'worries' on the whiteboard.)

The reason 1 say it's a funny one is because having worries is only sometimes a problem. Everyone has worries every single day. They are completely normal. But for some people, their worries get so big that they get in the way of being able to do the everyday stuff they'd like to do with family and friends. So if your worries are so big that they stop you from doing anything, you should tick this one.

The same goes for anger, and the same goes for sadness. Feeling angry and feeling sad are normal. They happen to everyone. However, if your rage becomes so big a lot of the time, you would tick this one. (Therapist writes 'angry' on the whiteboard.)

And if your sadness becomes really big too often, you would tick this one. (Therapist writes 'sad' on the whiteboard.)

Next, we have homework. 1 know we already mentioned school work, but some kids find that there is something about homework that just seems to cause a lot of trouble for them. (Therapist writes 'homework' on the whiteboard.)

Okay, just two more. If you have trouble organizing, then tick the next one. This would be for kids who forget things, lose things or can't seem to do things on time. (Therapist writes 'organization' on the whiteboard.)

And the last one is screen time! Most families argue about this, but I'm wondering whether it's a big deal at your place. (Therapist writes 'screen time' on the whiteboard.)

Okay, so bring your whiteboard marker and tick the ones you think might be problems for you.

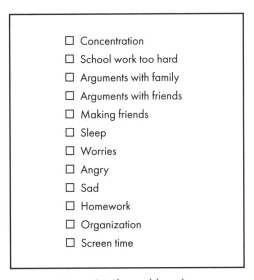

☐ Concentration
☐ School work too hard
☐ Arguments with family
☐ Arguments with friends
☐ Making friends
☐ Sleep
☐ Worries
☐ Angry
☐ Sad
☐ Homework
☐ Organization
☐ Screen time

Figure 3.1 The problems list

Note the language of acceptance and normalization that goes through the process, enabling the young person to feel safe, particularly around the descriptions of the three emotions (worry, anger and sadness). Note also the placement of these three emotions, which are towards the centre of the list. In this way, the more everyday issues appear towards the beginning and the end, utilizing the primacy and recency effects to minimize pressure.

Most children enjoy writing on the whiteboard and will approach the activity openly. Some will tick items easily and instantly launch into discussion around their various problems. It may be tempting to move into more in-depth questioning. I would encourage, however, documenting any details on the whiteboard (e.g. writing 'Sister' next to arguments if the child has mentioned this as a problem), to show that you have heard and will follow up later.

Children with greater reluctance may not tick anything or approach the board with uncertainty. Offering a half-tick for an item that is *maybe a problem* can reduce the pressure. If a child says nothing, a circular questioning approach could be attempted.

Therapist: If I gave Mum the whiteboard marker, what do you think she would tick?

At times, it may indeed be appropriate to give the parent a different coloured marker and ask them to tick the ones they feel are problematic for the child.

A photo can be taken of the whiteboard to emphasize that the responses are important and will be revisited.

Part 2: The people in my life

The second part of the session requires the therapist to gather as much information as possible about the important people (and pets) in a young person's life. A family tree (genogram) and friend map will be drawn in a way that provides extensive information. Young people typically enjoy participating in the process and watching the map of their lives evolve.

This is best completed on a double-sided A4 piece of paper, but it can be done on a whiteboard or adapted for Telehealth via digital whiteboards.

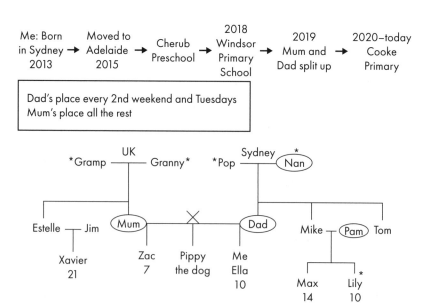

Figure 3.2

Therapist: I'd like to find out about all of the important people in your life. Let's start with the people at home. Who do you live with?

The child will easily name the people in their household. There have been no assumptions in the language about parents being together or separated, the gender mix of parents, or an absent parent. Children with separated parents will have the opportunity to describe their living arrangements. Note the left-hand box in Figure 3.2, specifying the shared parenting arrangements.

The therapist will begin a genogram that includes information about parents and siblings, including sibling ages. Pets are often very important to young people, so ensure you have asked about any pets and their ages.

The genogram is then extended to include grandparents, aunts, uncles, and first cousins (including the ages of young people), again being respectful with language. For example:

Therapist: So Dad's brother is called Gary. Does Gary have his own family?

This is preferable to *Who is Gary's wife?*

Noting the city where relatives live provides further useful data. For particularly large families, one can request to include only those relatives with whom the young person has regular contact.

For those children who have moved schools or cities, a brief timeline at the top of the page provides a quick reference to their earlier years.

Therapist: That's a lot of family. Now, I know we could go on and on with more cousins, but my goal is to have everybody in your family who is important and involved in your life. Is there anyone else?

Now let's turn the page over, and we are going to create a new map of other important people in your life (Figure 3.3). Friends, teachers and anyone else you can think of. Let's start off with friends. Friends are harder to map than family because the way we relate to them is not always obvious.

Let's start with people at your school. Some kids have a friendship group. They hang out with the same people pretty much every day. Other kids have one friend or just play with random people each day. Some kids have a bit of each. What is it like for you?

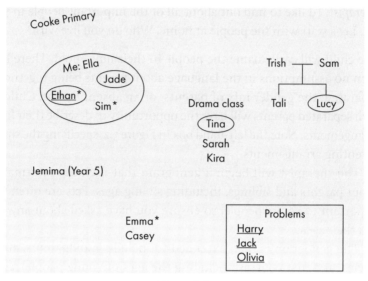

Figure 3.3

The therapist would start by creating a circle in which to place the names of the people the young person plays with most often. If they describe a group, the therapist would ask: And where do you go in the group? Are you inside the circle, or should I put you more out here on the edge?

Are there other people you sometimes play with or talk to? I'm not asking about the people in your group, but rather the kids in your class that you sometimes chat with. Perhaps you enjoy doing group work together. Anyone from a different year level? Sport team?

Are there any adults at school who are important to you, such as teachers?

Let's look at friends who aren't at your school. Are there any neighbours you play with? What about activities such as sports? Drama? Dance? Do you have any friends there? Previous schools? Online friends?

How about family friends? Perhaps friends of Mum's or Dad's friends and their kids?

Now the final section we need to put down is not so fun, but everybody has one. I call it the problem section. This is where we put the names of people who affect our lives, but not in a good way. Perhaps there's someone at school who treats you unfairly. Maybe it's just someone who annoys you, even if it's for no particular reason. There could be someone who is mean to other kids.

After completing both the family and friend maps, the therapist can hold up the double-sided paper and check the following:

Would you say that everyone who is an important part of your life is on this paper?

Now I would like you to take this pencil, and I would like you to place circles around the names of those people you can really count on. People who help you and are good to you. You can circle as few or as many as you like.

Remember both sides of the paper.

If somebody is a 'maybe,' you could give them a semi-circle.

The child is given a pencil to circle the names of any support people in their life.

Now I'd like you to underline the names of those people who can stress you out. Do remember that nobody is perfect, and it is quite possible for the same person to be circled and underlined because they sometimes support you but sometimes stress you out.

The child is given a pencil to underline the names of any people who cause them stress.

Finally, can you draw a little star above anybody on these maps whom you're worried about? You worry about certain people, perhaps because they have a tough life with lots of stress or illness.

The child is given a pencil to asterisk the names of anybody they feel worried about.

At this stage, the therapist will find plenty of information that may or may not require following up. Sometimes it can be useful to focus on one small aspect of the map and gather more information (e.g. I notice your friend Ethan has a circle, an underline and a star. It sounds like there's a lot going on with him).

You gave your sister three underlines! Wow! She must stress you out a lot!

Most importantly, this becomes a document that accompanies every session. We can explore various aspects during any future session that feels appropriate. During the first few sessions, it would be used as a platform for gathering a vast array of information regarding supportive or troublesome relationships. Further down the track, the document also assists therapists to easily recall the names of important people in the young person's life as well as those who cause them stress, reinforcing to the child that you know and understand the situations involving the people in their world.

Examples of utility several months after the first session:

EXAMPLE 1

Child: It's my birthday party in three weeks.

Therapist: How many kids have you invited?

Child: Mum said I could only have four friends.

Therapist: STOP! Don't tell me; I want to guess. Zac, Jake, Sim and Olive?

EXAMPLE 2

Therapist: What's the update with Sophia? You haven't mentioned her in a while. She used to annoy you so much.

EXAMPLE 3

Child: All the friendship groups are changing at school. I don't know who to talk to or where to sit.

Therapist: It can take a while for the groups to settle in Year 7. Are you still in touch with Ava and Lily from your primary school? You have always said they have been reliable friends. Could you hang out with them after school for a while until things settle down at your school? In the meantime, we can brainstorm ideas for making new connections in high school.

EXAMPLE 4

Therapist: I was just thinking about your pop. How's he going? Is he all back to normal after his fall last April?

The maps should be considered fluid documents, and updated friend maps are often necessary over time.

Part 3: Plan

By this stage, a therapist should have a good picture of what is going on in the child's life. The final stage of the session can be spent demonstrating your understanding and creating hope that things can get better. A third document can be created, entitled 'Plan' (Figure 3.4).

Plan

- ☐ Making more friends
- ☐ Handle Stella better
- ☐ Sleeping on my own
- ☐ Handle worries better (thunder, getting things wrong, giving speeches)
- ☐ Better at handing work in on time

- ☐ Anger management?? (Mum's idea)

Figure 3.4

This will involve the therapist suggesting therapy goals, being sure to reference the child's concerns, including the names of people they find difficult. The language of acceptance and compassion continues to dominate the mood of the discussion, so the child does not feel judged when suggesting where help is needed. A casual expression of 'we can work on that' brings home the sense of hope. The plan can be suggested entirely by the therapist, followed by the young person's approval. Alternatively, the plan can be created collaboratively. If the young person is willing to share the plan with a parent, this becomes a great moment to invite the parent back into the therapy room. Most parents find that the plan is consistent with their goals. We can also invite further suggestions from parents, being mindful of the young person's response. If they disagree with the parent's addition to the plan, we can write it towards the bottom of the page, marked separately from the rest of the plan.

By the end of this session, a young person should walk away feeling as though the therapist truly knows their world and believes in their struggles. When a child feels understood, a sense of hope typically follows. Most importantly, a child will be willing to return to therapy where they can learn the skills to create a valued and meaningful life.

Chapter 4

Neuroscience for Kids

Having established a welcoming, compassionate and fun therapeutic environment, therapists can turn their attention to the child's presenting issues. Psychoeducation around the impact our minds have on our reactions can open up enormous possibilities for learning. Understanding the role of the brain in relation to fear allows children to quickly make sense of some of their thoughts, feelings and reactions.

An ACT approach honours many of the well-established approaches to teaching neuroscience, while incorporating an emphasis on normalizing and accepting the cognitive and physiological changes that accompany the threat response. Introducing these concepts at the earlier stages of therapy has many benefits. For starters, it is an appropriate use of therapy time when working with children who are still reluctant to open up about problems. By introducing aspects of neuroscience in a child-friendly manner, the young person is able to simply learn a scientific concept, without the pressure of disclosing any of their personal information. When presented well and with compassion, the normalizing emphasis of the approach continues to build on the developing relationship between child and therapist. Child-friendly neuroscience can be equally appealing for those children who are already opening up in the therapy room. Most children will enjoy learning the concepts and will start to apply the information to their own experiences. Regardless of the child's willingness to disclose their experiences, they can be encouraged to notice their experiences. It can be tremendously beneficial to involve parents in these discussions to maximize reinforcement of the learning at home.

The fight-flight response

Therapist: I'd like to show you some really interesting stuff about worries and how the brain works. The brain has many jobs to do and today we are going to talk about one of its most important jobs: keeping you safe. The brain is constantly looking out for danger, so it can help you take action if you need to. Imagine that you step out on to the road and you suddenly hear the screech of a car racing towards you. You won't have time to think about a detailed plan, but you manage to jump out of the way really quickly. That was thanks to the brain!

Well, how does it work? When we feel unsafe, the brain kicks into action without us even noticing. It starts to organize our mind so that we focus on the most important thing in front of us – our ability to stay safe. That's going to help us solve the problem and get out of this dangerous situation.

First, the brain sends messages through the body that help pump the heart very quickly. That way the heart can send extra blood to places that we really need in an emergency, like our legs, so we can run faster, or our arms, so we can be stronger and protect ourselves. This is called the fight-flight response.

At this stage, visual aids can be used to enhance learning and invite more child involvement at a pace that is comfortable. The therapist draws an outline of a human body, indicating a heart, with paths leading out towards the arms and legs as described below (Figure 4.1).

Figure 4.1

The child is invited to add some of their own physical sensations while discussing the physiological responses during the fight-flight response.

Therapist: Do you notice any changes in your body when you are scared or afraid?

Parents may also be invited to indicate their own physical reactions to anxiety. This is particularly helpful if the child is reluctant to offer responses. A map of the family's physiological responses to threat can be created by giving each parent and child a different coloured marker. Typical physiological sensations that are noticed may include:

- racing heart
- dizziness
- tight chest
- sweating
- tummy pain
- fuzzy brain
- fast breathing

- trouble breathing
- red face
- fidgeting
- wobbly legs
- shaky hands
- headache.

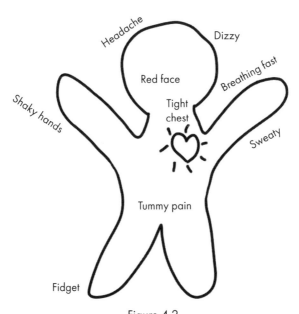

Figure 4.2

A discussion around which members of the family notice differing or the same sensations helps to reinforce the normalization of the threat response. It also creates a language within the family to assist them in discussing their own anxiety-based physiology more openly between sessions. From an ACT perspective, we are implicitly creating messages around normalizing and therefore accepting anxiety-related sensations.

Therapist: Whenever we feel worried or unsafe, the brain jumps into action and creates lots of changes in our body. That way, it saves us from harm by helping us be strong enough to protect ourselves (fight) or run away from danger (flight).

Once the child has understood physiological reactions in the context of a physical threat, we turn our attention to those times when the fight-flight response is activated when no immediate danger is present. These reactions are most common in situations that resemble threats, such as fear of being excluded from school.

Therapist: But what about all those times you feel worried about something that can't hurt your actual body, like worrying about a test, being left out or missing your parents? When this happens, your brain doesn't understand the difference between actual danger and mind worries. So your brain and body act in the same way as though they were being chased by a vicious beast! Even if there's no actual reason to run to safety, the body still does all of this stuff we drew on the picture (refer to Figure 4.2). The problem is that when the body changes in this way, some weird and uncomfortable feelings can show up and make you feel like your heart is exploding or you have to fidget. Some kids get a wonky tummy. Others feel like they just have to run away and hide.

The body changes can also move some blood out of your brain, making it harder to think straight. This can sometimes make your imagination run a bit wild and trick you into thinking you are in much more danger than you actually are. It exaggerates the danger!

The therapist could use this opportunity to ask the young person about some of their anxious thoughts when their brain is exaggerating the danger. It would be useful for the therapist to suggest some thoughts other children have to encourage more information. For example:

They all hate me.

I'll fail this test.

What if Mum forgets me?

An ACT approach teaches us to accept, rather than struggle with these thoughts when they show up. If we attach meaning to these difficult thoughts by assuming they must mean I am in deeper danger, then the struggle and consequently the anxiety grow bigger. This can be quite complex for younger children to comprehend and will be explored in detail in Chapter 8. For now, we will simply be asking children to notice these difficult thoughts and remind themselves that the thoughts could be the result of the brain exaggerating or 'tricking me' rather than an actual dangerous event. The act of noticing in itself represents the beginnings of our work on incidental mindfulness. While the fight-flight response can be overwhelming, we can teach children to pause and distinguish between a current safety problem and a worry caused by an exaggerated brain moment.

For some children, angry outbursts are the more pressing problem. Acknowledging the impact that the fight-flight response has on our anger will be crucial for these children as it begins to help them make sense of some of those reactions that can cause feelings of guilt or shame.

Therapist: For some of us, the fight-flight response can make us more angry than worried, causing us to do things we're not really proud of like blame, yell or hurt people we love. When this happens, the brain moves extra blood away from our thinking brain and towards our arms and legs, making us feel like we need to move or fight. This is when we might kick or yell. It can be hard to think straight, and we just want to move our bodies, scream or swear.

Normalizing the fight-flight reaction can assist young people in reducing the feeling that they are broken in some way. Society's tendency to continually impress upon children that they should be able to control their overwhelming anger serves to exacerbate those very fears when they come to mind. Recognizing that worry and anger are normal and that the fight-flight response happens to everybody can be an important early step in helping children unhook from the belief that their worries mean there is something wrong with them. When parents are available in the room for these sorts of discussions, learning is enhanced. More importantly, though, involving parents in discussions can reinforce the normalization of difficulties.

Therapist: Just remember, when your brain changes your body in this way, it isn't trying to make you feel horrible on purpose. It just can't tell the difference between a charging beast and a school problem. So, when you have these feelings, remember that there is nothing wrong with you. It's just the brain's way of trying to keep you safe.

A child-friendly video explaining the above can be suitable for certain types of learners and is freely available (Wassner 2021a).

Brainy deep dive

For older kids, or when younger children show an interest in learning more about the brain, concepts can be expanded to explore different functions within the brain. Most social-emotional learning programs that incorporate neuroscience make reference to the functioning of two broadly identified parts of the brain. These have been referred to in the literature under various names roughly referring to the prefrontal cortex and the amygdala, respectively:

- upstairs brain and downstairs brain (Siegel and Bryson 2012)

- mammalian and reptilian brains

- thinking and reacting brains.

Each of the above concepts explains the differences in our ability to function based on which part of the brain is receiving more attention. Explaining these concepts to children and adults alike can enhance their learning about our reactions to threats. Visual aids are crucial (see, for example, Figure 4.3).

Therapist: Let's have a look at two parts of the brain. Do you remember when we talked about the fight-flight response? Well, that all happens in this bottom bit down here (the therapist indicates the lower part of the brain diagram in Figure 4.3).

Figure 4.3

Some people like to call it the downstairs brain. The job of the down-stairs brain is to keep you safe. When you are feeling threatened or scared, it wakes up and sends you into action to help keep you safe. Remember how it pumps the heart faster to move blood around your body so you're ready for action? This is where it all happens. This is the part of the brain where fear, worry and sometimes even anger live. And it's not just a human thing, almost every creature on earth has a brain part just like this. It helps animals notice danger and take quick action to stay safe.

Now, this top part of the brain (therapist indicates the upper part of the brain diagram) is a little bit more complicated and is particularly busy in humans. Some people like to call it the 'upstairs brain'. It's the part of the brain that helps us solve some really tricky problems. This is where our *sensible* thinking works best. It helps us solve problems using facts and clear reasoning. It can also come up with some amazingly clever and creative ideas. This is the part of the brain that has helped humans throughout history to build houses, plan roads, write stories, invent electricity and create some amazing artwork, music and technology.

Another great talent of the upstairs brain is that it helps us plan and organize the things we need to do. It can help us to get started on our school work, work out tricky mathematics problems, get projects done, stay persistent, finish our work and give it to the teacher on time!

Once the therapist has described the many functions of the upstairs brain, it can be useful to pause and ask the young person about the strengths and difficulties they experience within the upstairs brain.

One could inquire about creative talents or academic skills. Separately from this, a robust chat about the young person's executive functions (including organization, planning, time management, persistence) can prove very useful. Often children are reluctant to discuss emotions but are willing to be frank about their organizational skills. By introducing this concept as part of our neuroscience psychoeducation, children may feel heard regarding their executive functioning struggles. These can be acknowledged by making a note of these difficulties with the intention to follow up with some executive functioning strategies at a later time.

Therapist continues: The brain is incredibly clever, but it can't do all of these jobs at once. So how does the brain decide what is important and what to focus on?

When we feel scared or threatened, the downstairs brain automatically gets all of the attention. This is great because it can keep us safe from danger when there is no time to wait. Imagine that a soccer ball is flying towards your head while you are chatting with friends in the playground. This is not a time to be thinking up a creative idea for your science project, so the upstairs brain is not really needed in that moment. Instead, it shuts down and gives all the energy to the downstairs brain. This is a great plan, because it's the downstairs brain that has the power to move you out of the way of that soccer ball really quickly!

What about all of those times when you feel really scared but there's no actual danger to your body? Like when you are worried about giving a speech or getting in trouble. The upstairs brain doesn't realize that your body is safe from harm, but it still gives its energy to the downstairs brain. So, the downstairs part gets louder, and the sensible part of the brain gets all covered up and muddled over and is harder to connect with.

The therapist can return to the diagram of the brain (Figure 4.3) and use a dark marker to scribble over the skills listed in the upper section of the brain. This is a stark representation of the fact that when threat levels are high, we cannot see or have access to those sensible problem-solving skills that the upstairs brain normally provides. It demonstrates that we are powerfully drawn to the needs of the threat response.

Therapist continues: Life can get pretty difficult when we can't connect with our sensible upstairs brain. It can be hard to make good decisions.

This is why it's harder to think straight when you are really worried or angry. It can make our worries exaggerate or make our anger grow.

It can make us insist on only doing things our way. This is because we are craving safety and our own ideas feel much safer. The problem is, it can cause fights with our friends, especially if they want to do it their way.

When we can't connect with our sensible brain, it also means that when our parents try to explain stuff to us, we might not be able to listen properly, and then arguments can grow bigger.

This is an important time to pause and reflect on what has been learned. When a parent is present, we can coach parents to demonstrate compassion and understanding. This may need therapist guidance in the early stages, with ongoing reference to the diagram.

Therapist: Mum told me about the fight you two had at the supermarket on Wednesday. She told me that you kept asking to leave the supermarket to go home, even though she hadn't finished the shopping. Mum thought you were just bored, so she insisted on staying when the trouble started. Now that we've heard a bit more about your side of the story, I realize that you weren't simply bored. You had seen a boy from your school in the supermarket, and that boy had been teasing you earlier in the class. I think that when you saw him, your downstairs brain went into action. You were afraid the boy would see you, and your worry got louder. I'm guessing your upstairs brain got all mushed over and you just needed to get out of there! So, when Mum tried to explain that she wasn't ready and you needed to wait, she was trying to chat with your upstairs sensible brain. That part of your brain was probably closed for business! All the action was happening in the downstairs brain, and you just had to get out of there. It was ready for flight! No wonder you yelled at Mum as she tried to stop you from leaving.

When we are able to assist the parent in recognizing the workings of the brain in this way and coach the parent to reflect on what went wrong, even in hindsight, repair can start to take place. This enables the child to feel heard and to regain access to the upstairs brain.

Mother: I'm sorry, I didn't realize Matt was in the supermarket. I thought you were just bored, so I continued my shopping. I know Matt has been nasty lately, and I can see now that you must have been very stressed when he was there. Next time something like that happens, is there something I can do differently to make it easier for you to let me know why you need to leave?

This also becomes a good opportunity to invite the parent to think of a time when they themselves made a poor decision due to their upstairs brain being offline. A simple example might be yelling at my partner when I am worried about something unrelated. A therapist can also offer examples to reinforce learning.

> I was so stressed about getting to my interview on time that I yelled at the guy in the car at the traffic light.

> I was so worried about my speech that I forgot to pack my lunch.

Even when the downstairs brain blocks access to the upstairs brain, we can still build the skill of noticing. Once we are able to notice that we are feeling overwhelmed or anxious, we can remind ourselves that there is a good chance our thinking is not clear. This simple act of noticing is an example of incidental mindfulness, which facilitates a small yet notable step towards better management of overwhelming feelings.

Therapist: Often, humans don't even realize which part of the brain is being loudest. But if you get better at noticing which part of the brain is working in different situations, you will find it easier to connect with the sensible part of the brain more often. Sometimes we can do this, even though we are scared at the same time. Some kids can even notice that it's happening and ask their parents for help. I'm not saying it's easy, but it is possible! And the better we get at it, the easier life gets!

It's really hard to make good decisions when the sensible brain is hidden. The good news is that once the downstairs brain has calmed down, we can reconnect with our sensible brain and apologize or problem solve for the next time.

A child-friendly video explaining this more in-depth version of neuroscience can be suitable for certain types of learners and is freely available (Wassner 2021b).

Once parents are able to recognize the distinct workings of the two parts of the brain, they become better able to navigate troublesome situations with their children. Chapter 11 discusses further uses of this concept with specific reference to parent–child conflict situations.

Summary

Psychoeducation around the threat response and specific functioning of the brain can assist families to recognize and therefore respond better to anxiety-provoking situations. This includes an understanding that the fight-flight response can be activated for both physical and non-physical threats. It can be equally powerful for imagined threats. Once activated, the fight-flight response narrows our attention, causing us to overly focus on the real or perceived threat, at the expense of our sensible thinking. An ACT approach to threat response contends that when a non-physical threat is overwhelming, it can reduce our ability to behave in the way that is most appropriate for us at the time. The language we use to understand this focuses on normalizing and accepting these bodily and brain changes. By noticing these changes, we are beginning the work of incidental mindfulness, better enabling the young person to relinquish the struggle with it.

Chapter 5

Mindfulness: Noticing and Curiosity

Mindfulness, or contact with the present moment, is a fundamental ACT concept that continually weaves through all other ACT principles. Mindfulness refers to the ability to pause and notice what is going on in our environment. This can refer to outer experiences perceived via our five senses or inner experiences such as thoughts, feelings, memories or urges. Mindfulness requires intentional focus and acceptance. While engaging in mindfulness, one simply notices and accepts their experience, whether pleasant or unpleasant, without judgement or attempts to change it.

Mindfulness meditation for children

Meditation is a popular method for practising mindfulness. There are many available digital recordings and mindfulness scripts that encourage young people to breathe slowly and notice their experiences through meditation. Some children enjoy these exercises and are able to truly slow down and better regulate after the practice. Mindfulness meditation has been shown to substantially reduce stress (Schreiner and Malcolm 2008) and is highly recommended for those children who are able to engage in it meaningfully.

There are many children who experience difficulties engaging with meditation, particularly when there are long pauses or minimal instructions. These children may better connect with meditation practices that incorporate a greater level of guidance. A body scan meditation guides a young person to notice different parts of their body. This can be a preferred version of meditation for children who might feel restless when simply focusing on breath.

BODY SCAN MEDITATION SCRIPT (WASSNER AND FLEMING 2015)

Let's begin by finding a comfortable position in your chair. If you prefer, you can lie down on the floor. Either way, make sure your legs and hands are uncrossed and in a relaxed position.

When you feel comfortable, close your eyes and take a long, deep breath in...and then breathe out. As you breathe out, make sure you blow all of that old, stale air out of your lungs.

And breathe in again, then out again, completely emptying your lungs.

Let's do that again. In...and out...

This time, as you take a breath in, notice how your belly expands as the air fills it. When you breathe out, the tummy gets smaller again.

Now you take a few deep breaths on your own, noticing the rise and fall of the tummy.

(Pause)

Now, as you keep breathing, I'd like you to turn your attention to your hands. What do they feel like? Are they hot? Cold? Maybe they're a bit sticky?... Try and think about whether your hands are touching anything. Perhaps they are touching your legs, the floor or each other... Notice the feeling of the air on your hands. Just spend the next few moments concentrating on your hands as you notice all of the feelings around them.

Now, as you continue taking your long, deep breaths, start to notice the feelings in your feet. What are your feet feeling? Are they tired? Relaxed? Sore?... Are they hot? Cold? Now think about whether your feet are touching anything. Perhaps they are touching the floor, or each other... Notice the feeling of the air on your feet. Just spend the next few moments concentrating on your feet as you notice all the feelings around them.

Now turn your focus to your tummy. Just think about your tummy. Notice how it gets bigger as you breathe in and shrinks as you breathe out. Try to picture the air as it goes in through your mouth, down your throat and into your tummy. And then follow it as it comes back out again... Really notice all the feelings in your tummy as the air goes in and out. Take a few deep breaths, really trying to picture the air going in and out of your tummy... Remember, as you breathe out, to make sure you blow all of that old, stale air out of your lungs.

Continue taking three more breaths in this way, in your own time. Remember, as you breathe in, to really notice it moving in and out of your tummy...

Now bring your attention back to your whole body. Let's breathe into all the parts of our body, starting with the feet. Imagine breathing a big breath into your feet, then breathing into your legs, then moving up to your hips, your tummy, your chest, then breathing into your shoulders, then your whole face, mouth, nose, eyes, forehead...and now breathe into your neck...then right down both arms.

Let's imagine our whole body again and return to taking a nice deep breath into your tummy...then out again and, as you do so, picture yourself in this room. Remind yourself where you are. When you are ready, open your eyes and have a big stretch.

When meditation is stressful

Many of the children who come to therapy will tell you that they simply hate meditation. They may find it boring or struggle to remain still. Some have negative associations with meditation following incidents of being forced into it at school, only to find themselves being punished for disengaging, opening their eyes or annoying others due to wriggling. Certainly, many neurodivergent children can feel deeply uncomfortable and vulnerable when asked to stay still or close their eyes. When a child is struggling with the idea of meditation, there are usually cognitive factors at play. Difficult thoughts related to mindfulness may include the following:

I'm so anxious, I can't even meditate.

I'm even bad at the simplest tasks.

There's something wrong with me.

Everyone's talking about how much meditation helps them relax. I need to relax more than anyone and I can't do it. It's so unfair.

Lying on the floor like this is killing me – how much longer do I have to stay still?

When the concept of meditation causes distress, we need to be flexible in our approach and find better ways to help children engage in mindfulness.

Mindfulness games are a wonderful way to introduce the concept of mindfulness in a fun and low-stress environment. These games encourage children to pause and notice their experience within the therapy session and set the groundwork for more difficult tasks in future, such as exposure, that will require noticing skills.

MINDFULNESS GAMES (WASSNER AND FLEMING 2015)

Mindful listening

- The therapist hides a ticking clock while the child's eyes are closed.

- The child needs to find the location of the clock by listening alone.

- Reverse roles.

- Adaptations: hide other objects in the room that have faint sounds (e.g. soft music).

Puppet time

- The child and the therapist both pretend to be puppets.

- Start by standing upright as though the puppet strings were holding you up. Slowly fold down each part of your body into a more collapsed position. Ask the child to focus on and really notice each body part as it collapses.

- Finish off with a shake and stretch.

- Repeat activities like a stiff robot.

Adaptations:

- One person is the puppeteer; the other is the puppet.

- Starting point from lying down

Mindful eating

To play this game, you will need three small pieces of food. Suggestions that work for this activity can be as simple as having a mint, a piece of bread and a sweet-tasting piece of fruit.

First place the piece of food in the child's hand. Ask the child to sit and describe what they feel and smell about the food. Examine the food like a scientist, judging how heavy it feels, how it sits in the hand and what shape it is.

Next invite the child to put the food in their mouth. The next stage involves letting the food sit on the tongue, once again examining its taste, feel and texture. Instruct the child to keep the food on their tongue for a short period of time.

Next allow the child to chew the food slowly, once again drawing their attention back to the properties of the food they are experiencing. Continue this process with each different piece of food. Ask the child what they noticed. Was it hard or easy to eat slowly? How did it differ from regular eating?

Finger switch

Ask the child to stretch out all ten fingers. Pretend to make the fingers fight with one another. Ensure they try to twist and cross over one another. Once they are very tangled, tell the child to stop and allow the fingers to untangle slowly, allowing them to float gently. Repeat the finger fighting, making sure the fingers are moving very quickly. Then return to moving them slowly, swaying and gently floating. Notice the tingling sensation.

Brain camera

You will need a picture from a magazine or printed from the internet. The picture can be anything, but preferably something that is quite busy, such as a train station where there are lots of people.

The goal of this game is to look at the picture for two minutes. Set a timer and let the child study the picture.

When the child's two minutes are up, ask the child to recall as many details as possible. While the child recites details, jot down what they say. When the child runs out of information, revisit the picture together and notice what the child remembered and what was forgotten.

Bubbles

To play this game you will need some dishwashing detergent and some wire formed in the shape of an oval. If you prefer, bubble blowing kits can be purchased.

The goal of this game is to mindfully blow the largest bubble possible. This requires significant breath control. When the child attempts to blow the bubble, most children will opt for the most powerful breath possible. Remind the child that it is controlled and consistent breath that creates the best bubbles.

Lego sort

A bag of Lego is poured out on to the floor. The therapist and child commence sorting the Lego pieces according to shape and size. For an extra challenge, this can be attempted blindfolded.

Incidental mindfulness

Incidental mindfulness involves deliberately pausing to notice our experiences, without judgement, during day-to-day life. If the child has negative associations with the word 'mindfulness', we can refer to it simply as 'noticing'. Examples may include the following:

- While walking down the street, notice the sounds in the environment.

- Notice the feeling of water on your back while taking a shower.

- Focus on the patterns in the brickwork on a building.

- When the smells of dinner waft through the house, pause and notice the smells.

In its purest form, mindfulness requires children to focus on one aspect of their experience, but many children struggle to do one thing at a time. They feel fidgety, restless or even anxious. Children can be encouraged to engage in a variety of activities that are not strictly mindful, though they incorporate mindful components by encouraging focus on certain aspects of one's experience. Some practitioners might argue that these experiences do not truly represent mindfulness and that children should be guided to sit with the discomfort of restlessness. Indeed, learning to sit with discomfort is a vital ACT goal, but the following examples should not be discounted as they represent scaffolded tasks to assist children in moving towards the skills required for pausing and noticing.

Examples include:

- yoga

- martial arts

- classical ballet

- pilates

- hiking.

These activities can provide the foundation for future skills that will become pertinent when we dive into the more complex work of facing difficulty.

Thinking about the five senses can be a more direct way to build a child's willingness and ability to engage in incidental mindfulness.

Therapist: Let's pause and name five blue things we can see in the room.

Can I ask you to hold this toy with your eyes closed? Use your hands to notice how it feels. Can you tell me three words that describe the feeling of the toy?

Let's take turns noticing any sounds we can hear. Let's see if we can start to notice tiny sounds that get further and further away.

Once a child has grasped the concept of noticing, we can begin incorporating the skills into the child's daily life. When there is resistance to working on difficult sensations, one can start with the positive aspects of a child's life. Bringing something we are grateful for to mind is a well-recognized strategy from the teachings of positive psychology. The benefits of pausing to notice those things we are grateful for are well documented and have been shown to offer a reduction in psychological distress and enhanced resilience (Waters *et al.* 2021). A child can be asked to write down three things they are grateful for, guiding them to mindfully pause and notice various aspects of their life.

Children can also be guided to use technology as a means of practising incidental mindfulness. Many smart watches have heart rate functions that can be incorporated into teaching.

Therapist: Let's take a look at your watch. Does it show your heart rate? Let's try to make the numbers go down. You can do it by slowing your breath. Let's watch the numbers fall.

Once this is learned, children can be guided to do it themselves during the week when they notice they are stressed.

Therapist: Next time that happens at school and you feel stressed, go somewhere quiet and look at your heart rate on your smart watch. See if you can make the numbers go down.

Many children complain that deep breathing 'does not work'. By incorporating their watch, they are more likely to engage.

Once we have established an understanding of noticing concrete aspects of the environment, we can move on to noticing more abstract features of our experience, such as thoughts and feelings. The child and therapist can choose a particular feeling, such as stress.

Therapist: Sometimes, when we are stressed, there are lots of changes going on in our body, like feeling sweaty or our hearts racing. Let's talk about that time when you thought you had left your speech at home, just before it was due. Can you remember what it felt like in your body? Can you remember any thoughts you were having?

Once the child has named the thoughts and feelings that accompanied the stressful event, we can encourage them to pause and notice their bodily experiences the next time they find themselves in a stressful situation.

Therapist: Next time you feel this way, I'd like you to just pause and notice what's going on. We are not trying to fix them; I'd just like you to notice which sensations are happening and then let me know next week.

Children are then provided with a home task involving pausing and noticing their physiological sensations when they next feel this way.

Once this practice is established, they can be guided to additionally notice their thoughts when a stressful situation arises.

Therapist: What was your mind telling you in that moment?

Once the child has developed the skills of pausing and noticing their experiences, they are ready for the more complex behavioural and cognitive work required to manage troubling experiences as they emerge in the future.

Summary

Mindfulness refers to an ability to pause and notice one's experiences in the present moment, without judgement. Mindfulness is a central ACT principle that directs us to spend deliberate moments focusing on our current experience, without being pulled towards future worries or dwelling on the past. Many mindfulness practices incorporate the use of meditation, which can be challenging for some children. Various strategies, such as games and activities, can be adopted to scaffold a child's willingness and ability to engage in mindfulness. Incidental mindfulness encourages children to notice their experience without engaging in a formal practice such as meditation. Incidental mindfulness can assist children in practising and developing the skills of non-judgemental noticing of experiences. These activities can provide the foundation for future skills that will become pertinent when we dive into the more complex work of facing difficulty.

Chapter 6

Values: A Vehicle for Motivating Change

Values invite us to consider those things that are important to us. Once identified, we can use them to encourage action that is consistent with them. In so doing, we are spending more of our time engaging in behaviours that move us towards a meaningful life.

Values are central to any ACT intervention. Being a fairly abstract term, 'values' is usually poorly understood by young people, so age-appropriate language must be incorporated. 'Stuff that's important to me', 'the true me' or 'the important stuff' are expressions that can be readily used. Some children like the idea of creating 'My Mission Statement', which describes how they want to approach the world. For ease, the following chapters will refer to this concept simply as 'values'.

Eliciting values

A successful values activity will explore the following concepts:

- What would life look like for me if it were truly worthwhile and meaningful, with the people that are important to me?

- What kind of person would I want to be if I were the best version of myself?

- What are the long-term activities that energize me?

Eliciting responses to these concepts can be tricky, particularly with young people. Many practitioners find it easier to start with concrete aspects of values before moving on to more abstract and complex elements. The use of visual aids, such as cards and drawings, may assist.

Values map

A values map serves as an easily digestible and visually pleasing setting for exploring a young person's values. A therapist can have a blank piece of paper with coloured markers spread on the floor ready for use. Carefully chosen questions will prompt the development of a colourful map that emphasizes what truly matters to the child. A relaxed environment should be created so that both child and therapist feel free to grab colours and add to the map. The map should be a little messy and, of course, changeable if needed.

A simple question that prompts a direct, concrete response is a great way to start.

Therapist: Who are the people in your life that are important to you?

Some children will name people easily as the practitioner and child grab coloured pens and start recording names on the values map. Other children will struggle to name people, so reminders from the practitioner can be helpful.

Therapist: What about anyone on your soccer team?
How about cousins?

A genogram or friend map created in previous sessions (Chapter 3) allows the therapist to offer reminders while also reinforcing to the child that they remember and are genuinely interested in the child's world and the people in it.

Following on from naming important people in a child's life, questioning is expanded.

Therapist: Tell me about things that you really enjoy doing; activities that make you feel good.

In addition to hobbies and fun activities, we also encourage children to consider those small moments they might enjoy with family and friends (e.g. laughing with Ella). Many practitioners have raised their own anxiety when young people mention a screen-related activity during a values activity. They fear it might be inappropriate to include a video game or a much-loved YouTuber on a values map. If the child has said it is important to them, however, we do place it on the map. It is not our role to judge the values of others. At this stage in the process, our job is to simply record what is important to the young person. A little later, we will look further into how we can tease out these values to determine which parts of the values-related behaviour are workable or not.

Finally, we come to the more abstract elements of value acquisition, in which we try to work out how the child wishes to be when they are being the best version of themselves.

Values cards

Many practitioners enjoy the use of values cards or checklists when discussing these with adults. Values cards are simply small picture cards that each state a value, in reference to how the person would like to be. Child-friendly values cards offer children a great opportunity to move about the room while gaining an appreciation of what is important to them.

Values cards examples

Being kind
Working hard
Being honest
Standing up for myself
Being friendly
Never giving up
Listening to what others say
Being patient

The children are then asked which of these is most important to them. One effective strategy for using values cards is to set up a scaled Importance Line from one end of the room to the other. Marker cards can be placed at opposite ends of the line, with Not Important at one end and Very Important at the other. Some children will need an explanation as to how to use the middle sections of the line in a scaled manner, and extra markers can help them through the line (e.g. A Bit Important). It can also be helpful to have a separate corner of the room with an 'I Don't Know' marker card. Children enjoy looking at the pictures on the cards and deciding what is important to them. We can then add the values identified at the Very Important end to our values map.

Values cards can be revisited in future sessions to extend the concept from self to relationships. For example, we could set up the values scale again and ask a child to place the values cards on the Importance Line according to the type of friends they would like to make at their new school. It may be helpful to assist a child struggling with perspective taking by considering the type of friend they would like to be themselves. The same concept can be applied to a child in constant conflict with a sibling or a child struggling to engage at school.

> If I could be the best type of sister, what would that look like?

> If I could be the best version of my student self, which cards would be most important to me?

My future self

Values activities for adults often encourage us to imagine our future selves as a means of assisting us to reflect on what might constitute a valued life. These activities offer an excellent opportunity to consider our current actions and reflect on how well they serve us in the long run and how well they reflect how we would like to see ourselves. They also provide a chance to reflect on our relationships in a more focused way. Children, however, lack the capacity to truly grasp the concept of being elderly. A 9-year-old boy can barely imagine being a teenager, so there is little point in encouraging him to imagine his death bed surrounded by his children and grandchildren. A more relevant version of this activity could be developed to enable children to reflect on various aspects of their lives.

> What would I say in my Grade Six leadership speech? How could I convince the students and teachers that I deserve to be school captain?

> Imagine that you are about to graduate from school and that you look back on all your years at school. How would you like to remember your time at school?

For those children who live within communities that have a rite of passage from childhood to adulthood (e.g. bar mitzvah, first communion, walkabout), we could encourage them to think about the speech others might deliver at the event. This activity further extends the values concept from self to relationships.

What would I hope that Dad would say about the type of son I am?

If my sister gave a speech at my 21st birthday, what would I hope she would say about the kind of brother I am?

What do I hope my friends would say about the type of friend I have been?

It would be especially useful to choose questions based on the child's actual experiences. For example, the 21st speech activity would feel far more relevant if the child had actually attended a 21st party in the past, perhaps that of a cousin.

In summary, a values map (Figure 6.1) can be created in sessions in a fun and colourful manner. The map should be named in a meaningful way that the child understands, such as 'Ava's Important Stuff'. This map can be kept and revisited throughout subsequent therapy sessions, as a tool to motivate behaviour change.

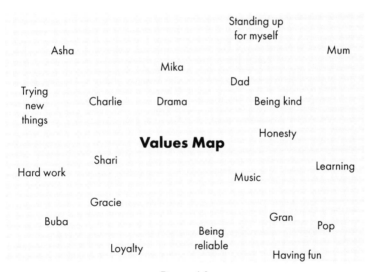

Figure 6.1

Eliciting values with 'concrete' kids

There are some young people for whom the abstract nature of a values discussion is not well understood. This could be for many different reasons, including, but not limited to, neurodivergence, intellect, or age.

A few simple questions can start off a rich discussion in which most children will willingly engage:

What do you really care about?

What do you love doing?

What do you really want?

The nature of these questions may yield concrete responses. For example:

I want more friends.

I care about my dog.

I want to worry less.

I want Mum to take my side more.

I love Netflix.

I want Mrs Watson to get fired from my school.

I want to be a professional gamer.

The above comments represent a variety of life aspects that present more as a list of wishes and grievances. While they are not values, they certainly provide a great deal of information about what is important to that young person. A skilled clinician will take careful note of these comments and translate them into values. For example:

I want to be a respected and respectful member of my family.

I want teachers to recognize when I need help, and then help me.

When I'm older, I want a job that I love.

I want friends who like me for who I am.

Note the transition from helplessness to hopefulness. Once established in a more values-friendly and functional context as described above, we can start creating discussion around the fact that these are things we can actually work on.

Therapist: We can totally work on being a kind and loyal friend.

Case example: Incorporating values into complex situations

Nina was a 12-year-old girl whose parents were separated. She had a long history of behavioural difficulties, often attributable to high levels of impulsivity. Nina spoke obsessively about wanting the latest technology, and believed that all the children at school owned better devices. Nina lived predominantly with her father and only visited her mother on an occasional basis. Nina's mother was often unavailable and had a tendency to let Nina down by breaking promises, including cancelling arrangements at the last minute.

On one occasion, Nina arrived at therapy with her father. It quickly became obvious that they were very angry with one another. Nina's father explained that she had been engaging in some inappropriate discussions on social media over the past few weeks. This culminated in Nina posting some tactless photos online the previous night that had social repercussions for her at school the next day. Nina's father confiscated her phone for five days. Nina was furious and unwilling to engage with her father. I asked him to leave the room so I could speak privately to Nina.

During our discussion, Nina informed me that she felt her social status was being negatively impacted due to her 'old' phone. She believed that her recent social media posts were not a big deal and that her father was exaggerating what had happened. Nina reported that she planned to move out of her father's place as he did not understand her situation. She added that she would move in with her mother, who had promised to buy her the latest iPhone.

Concerns came to mind regarding Nina's mother's ability to follow through on these promises. Concerns regarding the impact of Nina's recent inappropriate posts also deserved attention, as did the potential for future online behaviour when she regains the use of technology. Discussing these concerns with Nina directly, however, was unlikely to change her thinking or behaviour, as she remained hooked on her strong desire for a new iPhone and her right to continue posting on social media.

In previous sessions, Nina had completed a values map where she identified multiple values around respectful friendships and home-life stability. We had talked about the type of daughter she wanted to be, the type of sister she wanted to be and even the type of parent she would like to be when older. We had also explored behaviours that were inconsistent with those values, many around social media use. By revisiting Nina's old map, she was slowly able to unhook from her unhelpful narrow focus (iPhone) and think about how she truly wanted her life to look. She recognized the stability of home life with her father and noticed that in previous sessions she had discussed valuing her father's boundaries, even though they were upsetting at times. We were able to move around the map, asking questions about workability in the short and long term and continually referring back to Nina's core values. In this way, there was no need to enter into a logical argument about Mum's reliability. Nor was it necessary to rehash the trouble with social media. Nina was able to calm down and slowly consider her situation. By the end of the session, her father was able to return to the room, and Nina reluctantly accepted the five-day phone confiscation.

Action matching values

Once we have established what is truly important to a child, we can use this information to motivate behaviour change. Our first step is to recognize any discrepancies between a child's values and current actions. At this stage, we are not necessarily aiming for behaviour change, but we are certainly aiming to assist the young person in noticing when they engage in a behaviour that is not consistent with their values. We enable the young person to continue building mindfulness skills by introducing the concept of noticing within the values activity.

Noticing unworkable behaviour

When you believe you have established adequate rapport and trust with the young person, it is possible to help them start noticing when they are engaging in some of their unworkable behaviours. The following prompt can be introduced playfully and certainly without judgement:

Therapist: When you're in a really, really, bad mood, what do you normally do? Where do you go?

If a child is reluctant to offer ideas, it may suggest that they are not ready for this activity. Nonetheless, gentle encouragement should be attempted, with careful consideration of the child's responses to suggestions.

Unlike other therapies, such as psychoanalysis, ACT does make room for a therapist to engage in some self-disclosure. In fact, a crucial feature of ACT is normalizing struggle and difficulty.

Therapist: I do admit that I swore at another driver in the supermarket car park yesterday.

Therapist: When I'm in a really bad mood, I sometimes blame my wife for things she didn't even do.

Therapist: When I'm really upset, I sometimes just lie on my bed and refuse to talk to anyone.

A simple self-disclosure from a therapist in this context can assist a young person's willingness to open up about their own behaviours for which they hold shame.

Another method for eliciting responses from a reluctant child can involve the therapist disclosing information they may have been told by a parent. There are many ways to introduce these suggestions, and a therapist's knowledge of the child's relationships with parents will be crucial. Imagine a child who is known to throw items around the room when they are angry. Perhaps you know this information because their parents have told you so. Imagine also that this child has previously reported feeling more supported by their mother than by their father. Now consider the difference between these two potential prompts:

Therapist: Dad told me you sometimes throw things when you're angry.

Therapist: Mum told me that when Amy (your sister) annoys you, you sometimes throw the TV remote.

By referencing the parent by whom he feels more supported (the mother), the child can feel comforted in the knowledge that their mother may have told the therapist this information with compassion. This is further assisted by your acknowledgement of the child's side of the story (your sister was annoying you).

Providing examples of other children's responses in similar contexts can be used as an additional method for eliciting a child's willingness to open up about their own responses.

Therapist: I know heaps of kids your age, and some of them tell me they do some wild stuff when they're angry, that they're not proud of. Some kids break things or hit people. It can be so hard to control yourself when you're angry. Then, to make matters worse, you're the one who gets in trouble!

From here, we can create a list of those habits of behaviour that occur when the child is not the best version of themselves. If the child lists a mixture of thoughts, feelings and behaviours, it will be useful to separate these into groups, as this will prove enormously useful in future sessions. For now, we will focus on behaviour. If the child experiences difficulties separating behaviours from thoughts, you could say:

Therapist: If I had a little spy camera in your house, what would I actually see you doing?

This list of behaviours will become the beginning of our work on creative hopelessness.

Once a map or list of unworkable behaviours has been established, we can engage in discussion around whether or not these behaviours have actually led to positive change. The short-term and long-term benefits of a behaviour will be considered separately.

Choose a specific behaviour and ask the child: When you did that, did it get rid of the problem right away?

Often, the answer is 'yes'. This is a crucial step in therapy. Acknowledging the benefits of any behaviour should precede any attempts to point out its flaws. For externalizing behaviours, we can commence with a frank discussion around the fact that actions such as swearing, yelling, hitting and blaming can actually make us feel good in that moment. They can provide us with a sense of justice, balance, fairness and even relief.

For internalizing behaviours such as withdrawal, we can explore how avoiding something difficult provides us with a sense of relief.

Therapist: I'm sure you felt a lot better when Mum finally agreed to let you stay home from school on Tuesday.

Therapist: Those girls in your class sound really loud and bossy. I can see why it feels better to spend lunchtime alone in the library.

When a behaviour becomes unworkable

Once we have explored why and how certain behaviours have benefits, we turn to their downsides. An exploration of the long-term consequences of a child's externalizing actions will broaden the concept of a behaviour's workability. The following prompts may stimulate a rich exploration of the workability of certain externalizing behaviours:

> When you throw things at Amy, does it stop her from being annoying forever, or is she still annoying?

> Did the same problem creep back, or did your actions manage to get rid of it forever?

> Does it really get you what you truly want?

> Does that make for a better afternoon?

> Does your mother listen to you more when you do x?

> Are friends more likely to include you when you agree to play their choice of game?

> When you swear at Dad, does it help him to listen better and understand your point of view?

A recognition of the long-term problems associated with the behaviour cannot be ascertained without referring back to the child's values. If a child has indicated that they want to be understood, respected or listened to, we can point out that swearing and hitting generally do not yield the desired outcome.

Many ACT therapists use the term 'Away Moves' to describe unworkable behaviours. Children enjoy this terminology and can typically utilize it with ease. The Away Moves associated with externalizing behaviours can be easier to explore than internalizing behaviours, as unwanted consequences often directly follow the behaviour. A child who swears may have his screen privileges removed for the day, whereas a child who avoids socializing may not experience immediate unwanted consequences.

The concept of avoidance was explored in depth in Chapter 1. Avoidance can be classified as an Away Move. The long-term problems associated with avoidance are difficult to sell to a child who is reluctant to leave the comfort and relief that avoidance can provide. In order to prompt a reluctant child's willingness to recognize the problems with avoidance, the link with values becomes paramount. For the school-avoidant child to recognize the unworkability of their stay-at-home behaviour, we need to have established that perhaps learning and friendships are important to them. From there, we gently encourage the young person to recognize that missing more school days pulls them further away from being the type of learner or friend they want to be.

Children may feel judged regarding the behaviours being discussed, so it is important to deliver the discussion within a compassionate context, frequently acknowledging the benefits of the behaviour:

I can see how that feels safer and easier.

That was a really tough day for you. I can see why you did that.

Emma has been picking on you a lot lately. I'm not surprised you snapped.

When followed up with an appropriate discussion around workability, this compassionate approach will not be mistaken for an overly permissive one. The child may not be ready for behaviour change, but their recognition of unworkable behaviour becomes an essential focal point.

It should be noted that the workability of an isolated behaviour cannot be truly assessed unless its context is recognized. It may be tempting to generalize behaviours such as screen time as unworkable and exercise as workable, but this assumption fails to account for context. Exercise can be viewed as workable if the intention behind exercising is good health. There are, however, times when the intention behind exercise might be to avoid family time or, in the case of a condition such as anorexia nervosa, to avoid overwhelming negative feelings around body shape. The key here is to consider intention. When we engage in a behaviour with the intention of avoiding something difficult, it becomes an Away Move. If a child spends all afternoon playing video games to avoid homework and family interactions, we can classify that as an Away Move or an unworkable behaviour in the long run. If, however, that child has done their homework after a long day and enjoys using screen time to relax, then the behaviour becomes workable.

Children can be invited to notice any of their unworkable behaviour over the coming weeks. Therapists can suggest that they are welcome to try to engage in more workable behaviour if they feel ready to do so.

For now, however, we are merely asking young people to notice when they are engaging in a behaviour that does not help them. For older children, we can frame it as 'noticing behaviours that move me away from my values'.

A young person may return to therapy and report on an incident that occurred during the week that involved being in a terrible mood because of something that happened at school. The child may claim that when they returned home they were rude to their mother. This child may not have apologized to their mother, but the fact that they recognized this behaviour as being inconsistent with their values, an Away Move, is a huge accomplishment. There has been no obvious behaviour change at this point, but the mere act of noticing sows the seeds for more workable behaviour in the future.

Practical application: Noticing impulsivity

Many young people who engage in frequent externalizing behaviours can also struggle with impulsivity, yielding an additional layer of struggle. It will be important to compassionately acknowledge the added struggle when impulsivity has played a role in the behaviour.

Therapist: Yelling at people can just happen without much thought, especially when we are very angry. When we feel hurt by another person, these things seem to just come out of our bodies quite quickly.

Children who are naturally impulsive can especially struggle with engaging in workable behaviour when they are overwhelmed, so the noticing activity provides room for them to make progress in the face of minimal behaviour change. Impulsive children can be rewarded for merely noticing they are impulsive. This would only be effective with children for whom impulsivity has been a well-recognized problem that has been the subject of ongoing discussion. It also requires collaboration with parents and, most importantly, a discussion with the young person in which they express their desire to better manage their impulses.

Therapist: I know there are times when you regret what you do, like that time you yelled at your best mate Tom. I remember you telling me that you were so angry that you couldn't stop yourself. That day was an example of what we've been talking about – being impulsive. I'm going to try to help you work on that but for now all I want you to do is notice that you were being impulsive. Even if it happens afterwards, that's okay. So, for example, let's say you swear at Mum. The second you notice that it was another impulsive moment, I want you to tell Mum or even tell yourself, 'That was impulsive' or 'Oops, that was another Away Move'.

Noticing impulsivity can be rewarded. This can feel counterintuitive for a parent, particularly when the impulsive behaviour is inappropriate. Setting goals around 'noticing impulsivity' can assist with this. If a young person continues to struggle with the concept, it is possible to scaffold the skill by setting homework tasks around noticing impulsivity in others.

Introducing 'Towards Moves'

By now, the young person will be familiar with the problems associated with engaging in Away Moves. Thus far, we have not employed any obvious attempts to change behaviour. We simply encouraged the young person to be aware of when they engage in Away Moves. Behaviour change will become the next step in our process. When a young person engages in behaviour that moves them towards their identified values, we refer to them as Towards Moves.

When discussing Towards Moves, we are essentially asking young people to practise delayed gratification; to engage in a less preferred behaviour now, for the purpose of something more meaningful in the future. We are expecting them to be willing to experience a difficult thought or feeling, something unpleasant, in the hope of something better in the future. Many adults are unable to do this effectively, yet we are asking young people to have the emotional regulation and willingness to delay their needs. Moving in this direction can be extremely difficult, especially given the unpleasant thoughts (I can't do it; I'm not good enough) and feelings (anxiety, frustration, anger) that often emerge when attempting to move towards something meaningful. The following chapter will explore ideas for assisting young people to increase their willingness to relinquish short-term positive feelings for long-term benefits.

Summary

Values are a useful tool for motivating behavioural change. Values invite us to consider what is important in order to spend more of our time engaging in behaviours that lead to a meaningful life. The concept of values may be poorly understood by children. Fun and engaging activities such as values maps and values cards can be employed to assist children in identifying values. Once established, children are invited to consider the extent to which their behaviour matches their values. When such discrepancies are noted, children can be assisted to move towards their identified valued direction. The following chapter will explore ideas for helping children move towards this valued life.

Chapter 7

Behaviour Change through Committed Action

'Committed action', in ACT terms, refers to a willingness to engage in behaviour that moves a person in a direction that is consistent with a meaningful life for them: a Towards Move. Moving towards a valued life is not easy. More often than not, uncomfortable thoughts (e.g. 'I can't do this', 'it's too hard', 'I'm not good enough') and feelings (anxiety, sadness or anger) show up. When these distressing experiences become too powerful, it can be tempting to do whatever it takes to get rid of them. The quickest path is to avoid it altogether and give up. In previous chapters, we explored the trouble with avoidance, most notably that the problem usually returns quickly and more powerfully.

Acceptance strategies encourage emotional responses to happen rather than trying to deny or get rid of them. When engaging in a committed action approach, children are taught that they can have an emotion without trying to change it and still engage in what is important.

The power of 'AND'

The word 'and' can be a great way to start the work of taking action in a way that is both simple and easy for children to understand. Sometimes we hold unconscious narratives about whether we should do certain things. Our mind can tell us that if we are deeply uncomfortable, we should back away. The use of AND is one way to rewrite that narrative. Children can learn that they can experience something difficult and still move in the direction of what is truly important to them:

I can have a tummy ache AND go to school.

I can have an urge to hit my brother AND walk away.

I can get a terrible score on my mathematics test, feel hopeless AND still study for the next test.

Case example: Choosing to move in a meaningful direction in the face of discomfort (a)

I once worked with a very intelligent and conscientious 9-year-old boy, Matt, who excelled in karate. He had won multiple karate awards and been identified by his teachers as a real leader in the class, not just because of his karate skills but also because of the positive way he conducted himself within the group. Matt struggled to return to karate following COVID lockdowns. He held a constant nagging worry that he would sustain injuries during class. He worried about being kicked, breaking a leg or getting a concussion. Over time, he started to develop a fear that he would be so badly injured in class that he would end up in the hospital. His teacher and parents had chatted to him endlessly about the safety precautions taken in class, but Matt's fear did not seem to budge. Avoidance set in, and Matt's parents were struggling to get him to class.

Matt was guided to complete a values activity in which he identified strong values around learning, hard work, teamwork, persistence and respectful interactions with others. With great pride, he discussed his karate awards and his shame over letting his team down when he pulled out of a recent competition. He was also able to articulate many of the benefits of learning karate. It was clear that he really did want to be able to return to his class, but the fears had become overwhelming. Matt was invited to consider the possibility that he could feel fearful of karate AND still go to the class.

Matt liked to draw, and he had made some funny cartoons of dogs yapping at a young boy. Together, we developed a story of these yapping dogs, sitting in the backpack that he always carried to karate class. As Matt entered the karate building, he could imagine the dogs emerging from the backpack and yapping at the boy. The dogs would say things like:

Are you sure you're strong enough to handle this class?

Other kids get hurt all the time in karate.

It only takes one second for an accident to happen.

The louder the dogs became, the more they would pull Matt's attention. The more he looked back at those dogs, the louder they became. The dogs loved it when Matt gave them lots of attention. They started telling him what he could do and what he couldn't do. They would make Matt want to turn around and go home.

Soon Matt discovered that he could not stop the dogs from being there, but he could choose to give them less attention. When he didn't turn over his shoulder to tune into their comments, they were still there, but they did not get louder. Matt realized that he could not stop the dogs from sitting in his backpack, but he could choose how much attention he gave them. When he did not want to give them too much attention, he would put one foot in front of the other and walk towards his classroom. The dogs were still yapping away and trying very hard to derail Matt's efforts, but Matt had learned to let them yap in the background while he still headed towards what he needed to do.

A metaphor such as this can assist in building the language around a willingness to accept difficulty and still move towards what is important. Matt experienced uncomfortable loud thoughts AND he walked into karate class.

Preparing for committed action
Variability in personal capacity to move towards

Before commencing a committed action approach, it is important to help children and their families recognize that there is great variation in one's capacity to move towards identified values. This ability varies from person to person. It can also vary within an individual from day to day. When life is going well, one's ability to move in a towards direction can happen fairly easily and frequently. However, life constantly throws difficulties in our path. When we are overwhelmed with the tasks before us, it is far more difficult to move in a towards direction. Previous chapters have discussed the importance of meeting children where they are at within the therapy room before embarking on any task they may find emotionally challenging. This extends to any expectations we might have when it comes to a young person's ability to engage in a Towards

Move in real-life situations. Merely suggesting they sit with a particular friend at lunchtime to move towards a friendship-related value may not be enough to have the task actioned in the real world.

This concept can be extended to values that may have been identified around the type of person they would like to be. A child might have identified 'being kind' as a value they find important. On a good day, a child will find it far easier to behave kindly towards others. On a difficult day, they may be more likely to unfairly blame their brother or behave rudely towards a friend.

Individual differences in capacity to engage in committed action

Case example: Judging how much a child can handle

Ella currently enjoys going to school, is a relatively successful learner and has friends with whom she regularly plays. Sienna is the same age as Ella. She has some learning difficulties and is struggling with friendships. Both girls have identified that friendships and learning are important to them (values). From a perspective of committed action, we expect both children to desire moving towards school in the service of fulfilling this important stuff: learning and hanging out with friends.

Their capacity to move towards these values, however, is far from equal. Assuming other variables are essentially equivalent, one could easily predict that Ella would have an easier time getting to school each morning than would Sienna. Sienna would have a significantly greater number of challenging inner experiences (difficult thoughts and feelings) that she would need to manage to enable successful school attendance. We might also contemplate the likelihood that Sienna is engaging in avoidance strategies in the morning, such as procrastinating with the morning routine. One can readily imagine Sienna's parents' desperate attempts at reminders, task charts, bribes and eventual yelling. Despite this, Sienna's avoidance seems to win and the simple job of getting her to brush her teeth seems a relentlessly difficult task to overcome.

There are multiple strategies available to parents to encourage a good morning routine, and for most families, such as Ella's, these types of strategies are generally successful; a small reward, a little bit of scaffolding and Ella hits the Towards path with relative ease. For many of the young people who present to therapy, these strategies may not be quite so effective. Some of the parents I have met have vigilantly read parenting books and implemented these types of strategies to the letter, only to find minimal gains. This reinforces parents' despair and, in turn, increases the very struggle they are trying to manage.

Teaching parents to set expectations

In order to prepare a child such as Sienna to be willing to move towards her values, parents must recognize that their child is beginning the day with far more difficulties than other kids. A child like Sienna would be experiencing many more obstacles than Ella, just to get going. Brushing her teeth is not necessarily a simple task.

Parents can be reminded to recognize that an individual child's ability to attend school from day to day can also vary. Sienna could have days when it is easier to go to school. Perhaps it is easier on Wednesdays thanks to gardening club. Perhaps it was easier last month when she felt included with some peers. Perhaps it was harder this morning just because it was a grumpy morning.

First, parents are encouraged to step back from the struggles of task completion (just put your shoes on!) and judge how hard each morning is for the young person. Once established, expectations can be pitched according to how emotionally regulated the child might be that morning and engage in compassionate language that recognizes the struggle:

> I know you have sports today and that it makes you nervous.

> I realize it's Tuesday today, and you will have to see Ms Sharpe. Are you okay?

Once the child feels heard and understood, parents have a far greater chance of helping their child put one foot in front of the other, despite their distress. By now, it is hoped that parents have participated enough in sessions to have a sense of the child's identified values around school. Next, parent and child will need to expand their willingness to engage in difficulty as they move towards this value.

Finding value in something hard

Committed action necessarily involves the child being willing to engage in something difficult. For many, the relief of avoidance is a far more tempting path than persisting in the face of difficulty. Before we can expect young people to relinquish the delights of avoidance-induced relief, we need to find a way to sell the concept of delayed gratification. Traditional ACT approaches rely on reminding the person about their values as a motivator to engage in something hard. Children are far less able to feel invested in potential long-term benefits than are adults. Short-term motivators that connect to long-term outcomes can create the necessary link required for the child's willingness to engage in behaviour change.

Segueing to the long term: The short-term motivator

Seb was a 12-year-old boy who had been blessed with great natural abilities in mathematics. He had identified working hard as one of his key values and talked about becoming an accountant one day, just like his beloved uncle. While he could whip through mathematical worksheets with great ease and accuracy during class time, he had a tendency to panic during timed tests and had noticed that his grades were far better when there was less immediate pressure. In fact, Seb scored a D in his most recent mathematics test, whereas his class-based worksheets consistently graded him with an A. Around this time, Seb's older cousins were writing their final school examinations to determine their university opportunities next year. Seb's mind had started to tell him that he could never be an accountant because he would never be able to successfully complete examinations and therefore never gain a university offer.

Seb found himself sitting at home the following week, thinking about this Friday's mathematics test. His parents were surprised to find him disengaged and refusing to study. They reminded him of his dream to become an accountant in an attempt to connect the test with his goal. Seb, however, had disconnected from his accounting goal. With this disconnection came a generalization of his value (working hard).

Seb arrived at his therapy appointment the next day. The therapist was unable to gain any traction with his goal of becoming an accountant. She was, however, able to find some movement in his willingness to discuss the value of hard work. Gently, she discussed other people in Seb's life. They discussed relatives and friends he admired and explored their most appealing attributes. It was no surprise that hard working made an appearance. The therapist explored further, asking about the uncle Seb admired, and uncovered that the uncle displayed many qualities that Seb admired, beyond simply being an accountant. Slowly, the therapist was able to yield a values list that touched around the edges of the mathematics issue (persistence, resilience, hard work, courage).

By the end of the session, Seb was willing to engage in two small behaviours over the coming week:

- Commit to learning five words from a spelling list with which he has been struggling (persistency).
- Ask the teacher for permission to do the mathematics test in a private room (courage).

In order to support these two goals, the therapist was able to assist Seb in developing anxiety management strategies as well as distress tolerance skills and flexibility training.

Distress tolerance

Once willingness is established, we engage in the essential work of distress tolerance. Distress tolerance refers to one's willingness to experience something difficult. A young swimmer I was working with once told me that when she was doing laps, she would become annoyed by the waves and splashes of kids playing in the pool and swimmers in the other lanes. She reminded herself that she could keep swimming despite the splashes, creating a beautiful and literal visual of moving in a valued direction despite the surrounding difficulty.

An ACT approach says that doing hard things with clenched teeth or 'white-knuckling' takes away the acceptance part of a genuine willingness strategy. Rather, we are attempting to approach tasks because we truly want to, having understood their long-term benefits. We are reminded that we do not have to 'like' what we are doing and accept that it will feel uncomfortable. We are invited to approach the task with an attitude of openness, curiosity and willingness to experience some difficulty, which necessarily requires flexibility.

Marketing the value of flexibility

Flexibility is a key ingredient in behaviour change. In order to establish a willingness to do things differently, we first need to accept why routine and sameness can feel so good.

For most people, routine feels comfortable and safe. We often like to do things the same way, even in circumstances in which a change would have no impact on our sense of safety. A great example of this is the human tendency to choose the same seat. As a professional, imagine you attend a three-day conference. On Day One, you enter the auditorium and choose your seat randomly, possibly showing a vague preference for sitting towards the back or the front of the room. On Day Two and Day Three, you, as well as the vast majority of conference participants, will find that you have gravitated to the same seat chosen on Day One. The familiarity of sameness creates a certain comfort and most of us just feel good doing it. If you were to ask conference participants what they hope to get out of the conference, most would describe various aims around learning and networking. The chosen seat in the auditorium for three days can achieve the first goal, but that same seat would certainly diminish networking opportunities. Despite this, we continue to be drawn to the same seat.

Exploring the comfort of sameness makes room for an acceptance approach and should be established before challenging. At home, most children will tell you that they sit in the same seat for family meals, even though it is not a formal household rule. A therapist could then ask what it would feel like to sit in a different seat at the family dinner table. You would probably get an answer such as 'it would just feel weird'. Intuitively, humans are not wired to rock the sameness safety boat, so an intellectual appreciation of the value of flexibility becomes necessary. Fredrickson and Joiner (2002) demonstrated a link between flexibility and adaptability and enhanced well-being. Translating these findings to children will assist their willingness to explore flexibility.

The well-known spaghetti metaphor invites us to think about two pieces of spaghetti: one cooked and one uncooked. The cooked spaghetti is flexible. It can bend, move around and change when needed. When we choose to do things the same way, every time, we become rigid, like uncooked spaghetti. When the situation changes, the uncooked spaghetti breaks. Change is inevitable in life, and if we can only handle life in one particular way, we are going to snap, just like the raw spaghetti.

Changes in life are inevitable. People move schools and houses and friendships change. Those of us who are able to adapt to life's changes can manage life's hurdles as they emerge with greater ease. Flexible thinking helps us accept that change is natural and increases our happiness and productivity (Yildiz and Eldeleklioqlu 2021). Flexibility will help us adapt to new situations faster and experience less stress. Think about evolution! Flexible thinking also helps us find solutions more readily, as recognizing a wider range of options makes us better at solving problems.

Building my flexibility muscle

Although a child may now recognize the benefits of flexibility, their willingness to work on it may be lagging behind. A recognition of some typical concerns may assist:

> Doing something differently can make you feel anxious.

> Even if you know that flexible thinking is good for you, you may resist it because it feels uncomfortable or unfamiliar.

At this point, our previous work on values becomes central to the discussion. In order to create a willingness to accept difficulty and move in a more valued direction, we will need to establish a willingness to deliberately practise things that feel 'less good'. Children will present with varying levels of willingness, but we can provide reassurance that we will take it slowly by presenting the concept of a flexibility muscle.

The therapist first acknowledges how we can experience varying levels of discomfort and suggests that we start practising our flexibility with the easier ones. For example, 'feeling weird' because I swapped my usual seat at the dinner table is an uncomfortable feeling, but it is not a highly distressing one for most children. This is where we can start to help children recognize that different feelings have different levels of intensity. When the child has understood the value of flexibility, practising tasks that feel weird can be an easier place to start than practising tasks that carry a highly distressing emotional load.

Neurodivergent tip: Therapists should be careful when making assumptions about which feelings are the more 'difficult' ones. This is particularly true when working with neurodivergent kids. For example, anger is assumed to be a more intense or difficult feeling to manage than boredom for most neurotypical children. Many neurodivergent young people, however, find boredom an extremely intolerable feeling and will tell you it is far worse than anger. When commencing the work of distress tolerance and flexibility development, therapists should pay careful attention to the young person's experiences of different feelings when deciding which are 'easier' or 'less intense'.

SHAKIN' IT UP

Making a list of weird and wonderful ideas of how we can practise flexibility between appointments makes for a fun therapy session. Some ideas are listed below, but it is suggested that therapists create their own list with the child in session.

- Wear odd socks.

- Leave something crooked.

- Choose the second-best-looking apple instead of the best.

- Wear my underwear inside out.

- Start brushing my teeth from the top left instead of the usual bottom right.

- Sit at a different place at the dinner table.

- Suggest to my friends that we sit in a different part of the playground.

- Have breakfast before getting dressed.

- Use a different coloured Lego piece on my build.

- Put my lunch in a different container.

- Wear day-of-the-week socks on the wrong day.

As the list progresses, children sometimes lose sight of the purpose of the exercise:

What was the point of wearing my underwear inside out? What is that meant to achieve?

Remind the child that we are practising flexibility via easy and fun tasks that are silly in preparation for those times when we will need to be flexible for harder stuff. Once we get better at this, we can start building our willingness in other, more difficult areas.

Helpful thoughts to facilitate a flexibility task of medium difficulty

> Piano practice is definitely more boring than gaming. If I do a bit of practice now, it will make my lessons easier over the next few weeks.

> I can give up some YouTube time now and put my washing away quickly. Then I can watch YouTube without being hassled by Mum.

> I get really nervous speaking to the teacher, but I'll go up to the teacher tomorrow and ask how to do Section B. That way, I'll have less stress with the homework.

Pulling it all together

A useful way to convert committed action into a simple, user-friendly tool is via the 'Towards–Away' concept described in Chapter 6.

Case example: Choosing to move in a meaningful direction in the face of discomfort (b)

Sonya was a quiet and shy 9-year-old girl who had spent her first three years of school playing with one other girl, Tess. The two best friends did everything together. Lunchtimes were easy and play dates were easy. At the commencement of Year 4, a new girl, Becca, joined the school. Becca took an instant liking to Tess, who relished the excitement of a new friend. Sonya quickly became the third wheel and followed the other two girls around the playground. She was feeling left out and very unhappy. Sonya came to therapy and repeatedly discussed her wish that Becca never came to their school. When the therapist attempted to create some goals and values with Sonya, he noticed that she was unable to unhook from her one-eyed (unlikely) solution that Becca would leave. The therapist carefully considered the deep hurt and sadness that Sonya was experiencing. He acknowledged the hurt and started to subtly create a list of friendship values.

These values were placed at the Towards end of the values line (Figure 7.1).

TOWARDS-AWAY LINE

AWAY	TOWARDS

To have friends who include me

To be respected

Friends who listen to my ideas

Have fun

Friends who like the same things as me

Friends who want to do the same stuff as me

Figure 7.1

Sonya agreed that the listed values sounded great and was eager for Tess to once again fulfil all of these friendship needs. The therapist discussed ideas around moving towards these values with new people as well as with Tess. Sonya was not enthusiastic and felt extremely nervous about the idea of approaching new people. She was also holding very tightly to the belief that she could never find a best friend like the old Tess.

The therapist assisted Sonya's willingness and flexibility by introducing a triangle of friendship (Figure 7.2). At the very top we see those people who are our closest 'best' friends, and we usually have very few of them. For Sonya, it was only one person. On the next level down, we have other close friends. For most young people, it might be other people in their friendship group or a close family friend. As the levels go down, we describe varying levels of friendship through to acquaintance.

FRIENDSHIP TRIANGLE

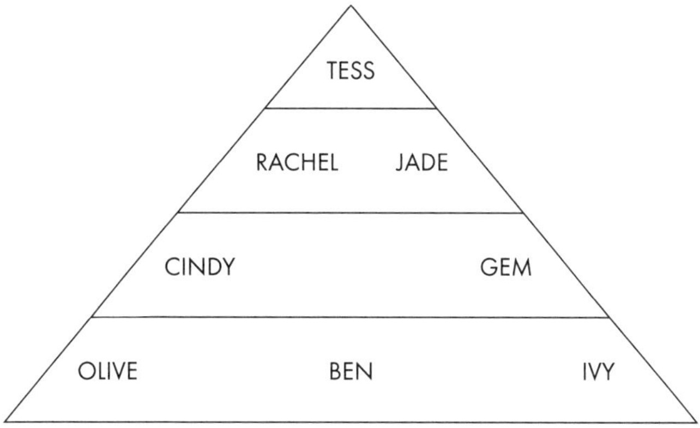

Figure 7.2

Sonya's therapist used the triangle to help Sonya loosen her belief that she could only have one friend at the apex of her triangle. The therapist encouraged Sonya to name people at each level of the triangle. It quickly became obvious that the middle levels were sparse. This became an opportunity to discuss the importance of moving towards our friendship values across various levels of the triangle. Sonya was encouraged to engage in small actions that could shift the friendship levels.

Examples:

- Choose somebody on the acquaintance level and smile at them as you pass in the corridor.

- Choose someone in my class who is kind but is not considered a friend. Approach them while you're waiting for the teacher and ask about a piece of work.

Once Sonya agreed to work on the tasks listed above with different people, the work of committed action could begin.

The therapist returned to the Towards–Away line and started to draw some small arrows heading in a towards direction (Figure 7.3). A discussion around moving towards Sonya's values had commenced. The therapist then drew a vertical oval shape that blocked the path of the arrows just before they reached the values noted at the Towards end of the line.

Therapist: So, let's imagine that tomorrow you decide that you would like to try our goal of striking up a conversation with Gem. You start walking towards her, just like this (the therapist draws arrows towards the oval). Now, you've told me that you are shy and very nervous about speaking to Gem, so I'm guessing that when you arrive around here (the therapist points to the oval), a bunch of difficult thoughts and feelings might show up for you. What might they be?

MOVING TOWARDS: UNCOMFORTABLE INNER EXPERIENCES

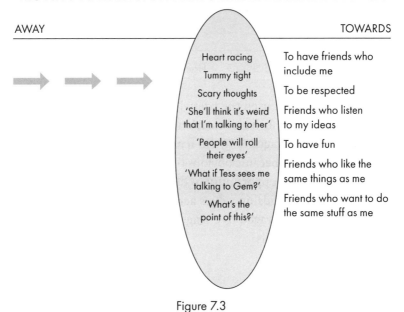

Figure 7.3

From here, Sonya and the therapist start to record any difficult inner experiences that could show up.

The therapist makes room for these thoughts and feelings, acknowledging how scary and tough they might be. In fact, they might become so overwhelming that Sonya could choose to give up and not approach Gem at all. The therapist would then draw the arrows turning around and heading back towards Away (Figure 7.4). This avoidance action typically results in relief, and it is important to acknowledge this and note how good relief can feel, compared to the scariness of being inside the oval of difficulty.

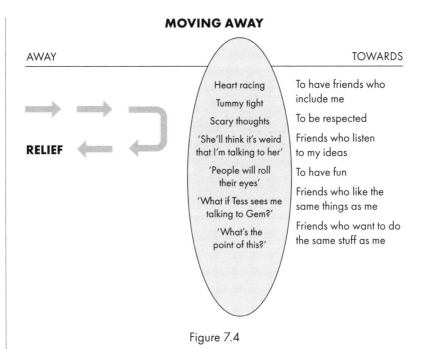

Figure 7.4

Questions around the workability of the Away Move next come into play.

Therapist:

Were you able to make more friendship connections?

Did the loneliness and frustration go away or did they come back?

Did it get you what you truly wanted?

From here, strategies around willingness and distress tolerance are ready to be revisited. A discussion around the fact that *anything* that is truly worthwhile does require some level of difficulty such as patience, persistence, courage or fear. There is no short cut and no way around the oval. We have to be willing to march through that oval to gain anything truly worthwhile (Figure 7.5).

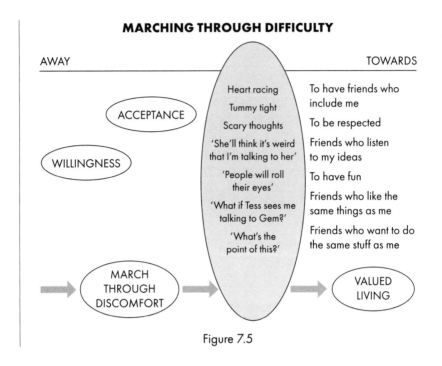

Figure 7.5

A video titled 'Avoiding It vs Facing It' has been developed to explain this process and is freely available on YouTube. It is suitable for children and can be easily accessed by therapists to enable them to teach experiential avoidance in a child-friendly manner (Wassner 2021c).

The following chapters will explore cognitive and behavioural strategies to support a young person's ability to march through difficulty.

Summary

Committed action refers to a person's willingness to engage in behaviour that moves them in a direction that is consistent with a meaningful life for them: a Towards Move. A child's capacity to do so varies from day to day. Parents and therapists can assist the child by helping them recognize their own capacity and obstacles on any given day through a compassionate lens. Building a child's willingness to be flexible can support their readiness to engage in important actions, even when they carry great difficulty.

Chapter 8

Working with Difficult Thoughts

Acceptance and Commitment Therapy offers a unique approach when it comes to managing troublesome thoughts. Thus far, we have discussed ideas for motivating children to be willing to face difficulty. We have explored the pitfalls involved in avoidance and highlighted the benefits of moving towards a meaningful path in life. Children may now be primed to recognize the trouble with avoidance and understand the benefits of accepting difficulty while moving in a direction that is meaningful in the long term. Putting these ideas into behavioural action, however, can remain extraordinarily difficult when undesirable, powerful thoughts show up. For many, this can result in giving up and turning away. Such avoidance may lead to short-term relief but also tends to make the original problem grow much larger.

Recall that in Chapter 4 we discussed the brain's tendency to focus heavily on any stimulus that is perceived as a threat, be it real or imagined. This is pertinent to review when discussing cognitions with children. We can respond to mental events (such as thoughts) as though they were real. When this occurs, our attention is narrowed and we are only able to focus on what is perceived as an immediate threat.

Imagine a young person walking into their classroom when they notice two girls whispering and laughing in the corner. The young person might assume the girls were laughing at them and become flooded with overwhelming thoughts:

Why are they laughing at me?

Do I look weird today?

Are they going to tell everyone else about this?

Do they know about my embarrassing fall in sports class yesterday?

A classic rational emotive therapy approach would focus on the evidence, asking the child for proof about whether or not they were indeed the victim of the laughing girls. In ACT, however, we resist the temptation to prove whether cognitions are rational or irrational. Rather, our focus turns to the fact that a threat has been perceived and the threat response has accordingly been triggered, narrowing the young person's focus. As the child is fully focused on the girls in the corner, their ability to think about anything else is drastically diminished. Indeed, they are stuck, or fused, with their thoughts around the incident. This could be referred to as cognitive fusion. When we are fused tightly with an upsetting thought, it can impact our ability to get on with our day. We become less able to engage in enjoyable moments or to carry out basic life tasks.

Cognitive defusion

Cognitive defusion is an ACT principle that assists people to defuse, unhook or loosen from powerful thoughts. In so doing, we are allowing the difficult thought to be there (acceptance), while still getting on with our day. We are not attempting to disprove or change the thought. Rather, we are noticing it and allowing it to remain as is, even though it may feel uncomfortable. In this way, the thought has less power to overwhelm us. Hence, we are minimizing the struggle with the thought and reducing its impact on our ability to do other important things in our day. We know that if we attempt to get rid of or avoid thinking distressing thoughts, they grow stronger.

Case example: Derek is coming to camp

Mack was a friendly boy in Grade 5 who enjoyed school and had no problems attending each day. Every year, the Grade 5 students would go on a three-day camp with the school. Mack had never been on a camp before, and the idea of three days away from home terrified him. His parents were aware of his reluctance, and Mack felt pretty confident they would allow him to miss camp altogether.

In the months leading up to camp, the Grade 6 boys started

WORKING WITH DIFFICULT THOUGHTS

chatting with the Grade 5 boys about camp. They described camp as 'the best thing ever' and said they wished they could go again. The boys talked about the adventure games, the meals, the cabins and even a special stop at a lolly shop. Mack observed the laughter and smiles of the Grade 6 boys, but his fears only seemed to grow bigger. On one particular day, a Grade 6 boy named Jed told Mack that the best thing about camp was making stronger friendships. He talked about the group activities and the need to work as a team. He smiled as he recounted falling in the lake with his friends and the challenges they endured together. 'It made us closer,' he said. Jed's words had an impact on Mack. Mack loved his friends and hated the idea of missing this opportunity to strengthen his friendships or, worse still, missing out.

Mack arrived at therapy and was quickly able to identify an important friendship value related to camp (stronger connections with my friends). His willingness to consider attending camp was starting to develop, but he was feeling overwhelmed with powerful cognitions:

What if I can't fall asleep when everyone else is?

What if I miss home? I'm not allowed a phone. What would I do?

What if I cry? It will be so embarrassing.

I don't know where anything is at the campsite. I might get lost.

Mack's cognitions suggested that his anxiety was high, and it was decided that some basic planning and problem solving would take place before working with the cognitions. Teachers were able to answer some of Mack's basic questions about the camp, such as its location and daily schedules. This subsequently enabled a better focus on those cognitions associated with anxious rumination, most notably the 'what ifs'.

During therapy, we created an imaginary character whom Mack named 'Derek'. Derek's job was to try to stop Mack from going to camp. Every time Mack thought about camp, Derek would take over his mind very quickly and loudly:

You'll never get through camp.

• 117 •

You'll embarrass yourself at drop-off.

You won't have any of your friends in your cabin.

The food will be disgusting.

You'll never be able to sleep.

Mack was reminded that Derek had only one job: to keep Mack at home. Derek lacked any ability to think about anything apart from his one job. He certainly had no interest in Mack's desire to grow friendships through participation at camp. Unfortunately, Derek had no intention of relinquishing his role. Mack would need to find a way to attend camp with Derek.

Derek became a personalized version of cognitive defusion. Mack was able to gain some distance from his thoughts by attributing them to Derek, rather than having them be the fused truth in his mind. When Derek became too loud, Mack was able to use some helpful thoughts to keep focused on his goal of attending camp:

Hey, Derek, can you give it a rest today? I'm going to camp.

The food might be awful, but at least I'll have my buddies – we'll laugh about it!

Night time will be hard, but it's worth it.

Even if stuff is hard, at least we are all in it together.

As camp drew closer, Mack created specific cognitions to assist him in managing situations that were predicted to be difficult. He planned to imagine Derek sitting on his shoulder, spouting fears as he walked on to the camp bus. He planned to continue walking on to the bus even though Derek would be attempting to derail him. Mack planned to ask a friend to sit with him on the bus to reinforce his capacity to connect with his friendship value as he entered the bus.

At no point did Mack attempt to get rid of Derek, for this would have deepened his struggle. When our goal is to reduce difficult thoughts or feelings, we can find ourselves trapped in struggle. The more we crave anxiety reduction, the more powerful anxiety becomes. By enlisting language around allowing Derek to accompany Mack on camp rather than leaving him at home, he was making room for the difficult thoughts. If we simply threw Derek off the bus, the chances are he would return more loudly.

Mack did attend camp successfully. On his return, he described moments when Derek was quieter, making Mack's day easier and more enjoyable. The debriefing around this reduction is an important moment in ACT education. When we do achieve a reduction in the difficult thoughts (Derek's commentary), it is important to refer to them as a bonus that can sometimes accompany acceptance, rather than a goal in itself. The true ACT goal was getting to camp and participating with his friends. To get there, Mack needed to accept that Derek would often accompany his journey.

After a successful camp, Mack noticed that his worry was shifting to new things. First, he described feeling worried about spooky creatures at night. The groundwork for cognitive defusion had been laid thanks to camp. Mack was able to create new helpful thoughts in the spirit of Derek to help him unhook from the intensity of the worrisome thoughts.

Hey, Derek, are you getting bored without me? What are you going to hassle me about next?

Derek is hanging out on my bed again, telling me about spooky creatures.

The Derek concept was then expanded to include more playful strategies. Mack would picture Derek dressed up in humorous outfits related to his fear. Mack enjoyed imagining Derek arriving in his room in various spooky outfits. He still held fears about spooky creatures, but the defusion technique enabled him to gain enough distance from the thoughts that he could continue spending his evening in a way he enjoyed.

A few weeks later, Mack's spooky worries diminished, but a new worry appeared. Mack started worrying that he might be smelly and not know it. Sure enough, imaginings of Derek were created that involved brown patches on his clothes and green 'stinky' cartoon squiggles. Derek had become a representation of Mack's exaggerated worries. Derek enabled Mack to defuse from his worries so that they had less power over him. Mack could notice Derek and choose how much attention he would give him.

It should be noted that at no point were Mack's fears dismissed or ridiculed. They were first compassionately explored in therapy and only became playful when Mack was willing and able to identify that they were exaggerated and interfering with life.

Worry habits

A worry habit is a cognitive defusion technique that can be used to assist young people in recognizing common themes in their worries. All humans have themes in their fears. We often find that we have predictable triggers that can set us off. Common worry habits in adults might include:

I'm not good enough.

Fear of running late.

Worry that people think I'm stupid/I'm fat.

Nobody takes me seriously.

I must get this perfectly right.

When we take the time to identify our own worry habits, we improve our ability to notice them when they show up. Once we are able to recognize our own worry habits, we acquire some space or defusion from their impact. For example, a young adult may hold a long-standing belief that she is stupid. During her first day at a new job, she might carry out a task incorrectly. That belief or worry habit would likely show up very quickly. If she were able to pause and recognize that the 'I'm stupid' thought is one of her long-standing worry habits, she might just gain enough distance from the thought (cognitive defusion) to enable her to get on with her work. In this way, we are acknowledging that the true problem here is the process of the worry, or how this particular worry functions for this employee, rather than the content of the worry. In other words, she can recognize that the thought showed up because it's a habit, rather than due to any stupidity on her part. Thus we can focus on managing how the anxiety works rather than getting hooked on the actual content of the worry.

Children are familiar with the concept of a habit and enjoy applying it to their fears. Explaining the idea of worry habits should be light and fun, and it should only be carried out once rapport is well established and the child has already spoken openly about their fears in previous sessions. Therapists should be mindful that cognitive defusion is a playful technique that can be perceived as teasing if not handled in the appropriate context.

When explaining how worry habits work, it is preferable to include a parent in the discussion to assist with normalization. A therapist could also choose to disclose one of their own worry habits to reinforce normalization. If a child struggles to identify one of their own worry habits, it can be useful to explore fears raised in previous sessions from which the therapist could elicit a theme. For example, a child might have previously identified that they worry about robbers, fires and being in a car crash. Once brought together, we can suggest that this child has a safety worry habit.

The therapist then explains how worry habits work. Two important points should be made and written up clearly for the child to see.

1. Worry habits exaggerate the danger.

    For younger children, who might not understand 'exaggerate', one could say, 'trick me into thinking I'm in huge danger'.

2. Worry habits grow bigger at night.

    One person's worry habit is then chosen to illustrate the above. Let us use the example of the child with safety worries. We could coin it the 'I'm Not Safe' worry habit.

Therapist: When you start worrying that a robber might come into your house, you could remind yourself that the reason that thought popped into your head is because it's your worry habit. Our mind has thousands of thoughts every day. That safety worry habit pops into your mind very often! So, when you hear a weird noise in the house, I'm not surprised that your mind assumes it must be a robber. Your mind is so used to having that thought.

This explanation does not attempt to address the likelihood of a robber being in the house. Rather, it acknowledges how this young person's mind has a tendency to work; it has a well-established habit of assuming there is a robber. The child's mind has exaggerated the danger. From here, we can start to develop some helpful thoughts in the spirit of cognitive defusion, for the child to practise when the worry appears.

There's a noise... Obviously, my worry habit brain assumes it's a robber.

I'm worrying about safety again – how original, mind! Can you think of something different for once?

The second feature of worry habits (grow bigger at night) could be used to expand the concept of cognitive defusion. We can explore whether the safety worries do become more prominent at night. When this happens, we can enlist further helpful thinking:

The reason I'm having this thought is because it's night-time. Hello, safety worry habit! Of course, you've turned up as it gets darker.

Case example: Worry habits for values work

Let us consider 10-year-old Tom, who loves swimming in the pool but is reluctant to swim at the beach for fear of being attacked by a shark. Tom comes from a family of sun-lovers and most holidays are spent at the beach. Tom usually spends the long beach days sitting on the sand, watching everybody else enjoy the water. Tom would love to join them, but he is so terrified of sharks that he can barely approach the shore. Tom arrived reluctantly for therapy, concerned that he would be forced to swim in the ocean after the session. Through gentle discussion, Tom was able to describe the sheer terror he felt in his body when he thought about swimming in the ocean. Tom knew that shark attacks were rare but could not stop thinking that he would end up being that rare victim should he venture into the ocean. Tom spoke warmly about his family's holidays and smiled as he discussed the fun times they had. He spoke of his love of swimming and playing with his siblings in the pool. A swimming pool was not available at their most recent holiday, so Tom did not swim at all. Tom commented that he would watch the other kids swimming in the ocean with great incredulity. He could not fathom how relaxed they were in the ocean. He longed to be just like them.

The values work in previous sessions yielded rich information about how much Tom valued having fun with his family, especially in the summer. Having established his desire to be able to swim in the ocean, it was time to look at Tom's thoughts. Tom disclosed the following cognitions:

A shark could come and bite me.

You don't know what's in the murky water.

What if a shark came to the beach and nobody noticed until it was too late?

Brought together, these thoughts became known as the 'Shark Worry Habit'. Once established, cognitive techniques became easier to discuss. First, Tom was reminded that worry habits exaggerate the danger. Tom eventually became willing to try entering the shallow end of the water. We predicted that the shark worry habit would indeed show up. Tom persisted and entered the shallow end of the water, bringing to mind his values around enjoying swimming with the family. As predicted, the shark worries did show up. Tom was able to remind himself that the reason he was worried about sharks in that moment was completely unrelated to the likelihood of there being a shark. Rather, by noticing the thought and framing it as a worry habit, he was able to gain some distance from the thought and have a wider perspective. He could remind himself that the shark worry turned up in this moment because it is a long-standing worry habit *for him.*

For older children, we can expand worry habit concepts to incorporate references to the upstairs and downstairs brain as discussed in Chapter 4.

Case example: Worry habits as defusion

Saskia was an 11-year-old girl who was constantly worried about being attacked by zombies. Her parents had spent many nights at the end of her bed, reassuring her that zombies were not real. Saskia was bright, articulate and communicated very clearly that she knew zombies did not exist. Despite this knowledge on an academic level, she could not help feeling terrified of zombies at bedtime. We coined the problem the 'Zombie Worry Habit'. We discussed how problems can seem bigger at night for people of all ages. Sometimes we lie in bed at night, unable to sleep due to being stressed about a problem. Often, however, the problem appears much smaller in the morning. This is true for both adults and children. We then connected this knowledge to the neuroscience covered in previous sessions. Saskia knew zombies did not exist, but this information was stored in her upstairs or sensible brain. At night, when the lights go out, Saskia's access to the upstairs brain is minimized and her downstairs brain is on high alert. Add to this the fact that Saskia had a long-standing zombie worry habit and we can certainly see why the zombie worry was showing up as often as it did. Once this psychoeducation was established, Saskia was able to come up with some helpful thoughts consistent with cognitive defusion:

Good evening, zombie worry! Right on time tonight!

My brain is tricking me into thinking about zombies again.

It's just the zombie worry habit.

Mum just switched off the light and...cue zombie worry habit! Right on time, buddy.

Getting playful with cognitive defusion

Many therapists use cognitive defusion with great humour. Techniques that make light of difficult thoughts are often used as a method for unhooking or gaining some distance from an overwhelming thought. Many children are visual learners, so a character or picture of the worry can be used to start playing with it. In Saskia's example above, she chose to draw a picture of a zombie dressed up in a ballerina tutu. By picturing a funny zombie, she was better able to unhook from the image of a more frightening zombie. She saw this as another small technique to help her feel a little less overwhelmed when the zombie worries predictably showed up.

Songs and poems can also be created in the context of cognitive defusion. A child might choose to write down their unhelpful thoughts and then transform those words into the tune of a silly song. For example, when Saskia was being flooded with unhelpful zombie thoughts, she chose to insert her unhelpful thoughts into the tune of 'Twinkle, Twinkle, Little Star':

What if there's a zombie here?

What if Mummy cannot hear?

Zombie, do not eat me now.

Are you real? I don't know how.

Zombie, are you really here?

Please don't eat my nose or ear.

Obviously, it's important to keep in mind that making a silly song out of a young person's sad thoughts needs to be done carefully. Therapists must ensure that the child understands that the goal of the technique is to remove some of the power from the upsetting thoughts. It is crucial to ensure the child understands that it is in no way making fun of their troubling thoughts.

Thoughts are not always true

We have already learned that thoughts can be very powerful. When a thought pulls our attention by showing up frequently, we often assume that it must be true. Psychoeducation around how or why thoughts show up needs to incorporate the fact that, at times, completely untrue thoughts take up much of our attention. Children can be reminded of the following:

- All humans experience difficult thoughts.
- All thoughts are normal.
- All thoughts pass.
- Some thoughts show up very often, but that doesn't make them true.

When we are able to pause and notice our thoughts, we are engaging in incidental mindfulness. Strategies can be utilized to assist children in seeing that these are simply thoughts that can do no harm. Figure 8.1 can be used to demonstrate the idea of thoughts flowing through our mind.

THOUGHTS FLOWING THROUGH

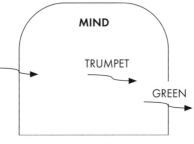

Figure 8.1

Therapist: I'd like you to imagine that this is your mind. All day long, thoughts are flowing through. They come in and they go out. Hmm, I must remember to practise trumpet later. There goes the trumpet thought through my mind. Pretty soon it will flow out again and I won't think about trumpet. Thoughts just come and go all day long. In fact, I can actually plant a thought inside your mind right now. Watch this: I'm going to tell you that my favourite colour is green. There goes the green thought – you're thinking about me liking green, and then fairly soon it will flow out again.

Now, there are some thoughts that flow in and out fairly easily. Others, however, kind of get stuck on the journey, and it's as though they land on little hooks in the mind. Once a thought is stuck on a hook, it behaves a bit like a magnet, and bunches of difficult thoughts start to clump on to it. When this happens, we can feel pretty rotten (see Figure 8.2).

What are the types of thoughts that get stuck for you? The child is encouraged to think about the types of thoughts that stick around more often. These thoughts should be written on the hooks in the diagram. The therapist can suggest that certain types of thoughts are more likely to stick around, such as things that are particularly important to us or worry habits. This would be a useful time to provide an example of a sticky thought.

Therapist: Think about the time when your family went down to the beach and were begging you to go into the surf with them. I'm guessing that shark worry was going through your mind. I can't imagine that flowed out very easily. I reckon it would have gotten stuck in your mind for quite a while (the therapist writes 'sharks' on the hook).

MIND HOOKS

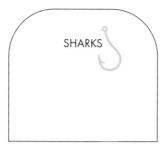

Figure 8.2

Can I tell you something about what happens to me when I go to the beach? Shark thoughts don't hook me at all, but I do have my own worry habit when I go to the beach. I really want peace and quiet when I'm at the beach, so I worry about other people being too loud near me. If this were my diagram, you'd see all sorts of thoughts about loud people getting stuck on my hooks. I can't see any loud people on your hooks.

Now, I have two questions: Out of the two of us, who is more likely to get attacked by a shark? And who is more likely to be sitting near noisy people? Neither of us! We are equal.

The fact that you have more shark thoughts than I do doesn't mean that you have a greater chance of getting attacked by a shark. The same is true for me. The fact that I'm busy thinking about loud people doesn't mean there will actually be loud people at the beach. The thought is hooked because it's one of my worry habits.

Did you know that when thoughts get really stuck in our minds for too long, they can trick us into assuming that they must be true? So, the more shark thoughts you have, the more likely you are to believe that sharks must be a true problem at the beach.

What if I told you that just because the thought has been in your mind for a long time doesn't mean it's actually true? The opposite is also true; sometimes thoughts that are absolutely true don't get stuck at all. They just flow through anyway. Guess what? It is 100 per cent true that I love the colour green, but I'm guessing that thought flowed out of your mind a long time ago! Just because we think about something a lot doesn't mean it's true.

There can also be times when we attach unnecessary meaning to a thought, particularly about ourselves, creating an overwhelm that is far more difficult to manage. I recall seeing 8-year-old Jayden in therapy, whose mother had recently given birth. Jayden was excited about having a little sister and became quite the happy helper at home. One evening, his mother was enjoying a cup of tea. Jayden looked at the boiling tea and, for a fleeting moment, thought about how easily he could pour boiling tea on to his baby sister and scald her. Jayden became frightened at his thought. He could not believe such a terrible thought had crossed his mind. Various thoughts passed through his mind rapidly:

What does this say about me? Am I a psycho?

What if I secretly want to kill my sister?

I'm a terrible person.

Mum should send me away to live with Gran.

A good brother wouldn't think this.

Over the following weeks, Jayden started withdrawing at home. He no longer played with his sister and spent more time alone in his room. Jayden had unknowingly attached meaning to the above thoughts. Indeed, the meaning he attached was far from true. He assumed, however, that the thought of burning his sister meant something about the type of person he was.

Jayden was reminded that our minds have thousands of thoughts every day. Many are useful. Some are just plain wacky and unexpected. When we attach meaning to a thought, it can pull us away from a meaningful life. In Jayden's situation, it pulled him away from the strong values he held about the type of brother he would like to be. Through cognitive defusion, Jayden was able to unhook from these thoughts. He was able to learn that not all thoughts are true and reconnect with his family.

Self as context

Self as context is an ACT principle that can further facilitate acceptance and defusion techniques. The concept is often poorly understood by adults, so adapting it for children requires careful contemplation. It is therefore recommended that it only be incorporated into therapeutic work with children once techniques of acceptance and cognitive defusion are understood.

Self as context can be understood via two key features: how I view myself (my conceptualized self) and my ability to observe myself as though I were an outsider looking in.

My conceptualized self

Conceptualized self refers to the views and beliefs we hold about ourselves. An example might be 'I'm the black sheep of the family'. Often we hold tightly to these beliefs, entangling them with other beliefs until we consider them to be literal truths. When the beliefs begin to impact life in a negative way, we need to learn to notice them so we can untangle from their power. Adults can be guided to recognize that our perception of ourselves is often skewed as a result of the stories that we tell ourselves. We can learn to step outside these beliefs and think about ourselves more flexibly.

While adults often hold long-standing and rigid beliefs about themselves, a child's sense of self is still developing. Children are very impressionable and can quickly acquire their self-views based on the comments of the people around them. This provides us with a bittersweet situation. On the one hand, children continue to gain some unhelpful self-views from others in their environment, such as family, teachers and peers. New beliefs can be latched on to and strongly held, very quickly and easily. On the other hand, their beliefs are still developing, providing an opportunity to encourage flexibility before the beliefs become too deeply entrenched. Referring to these beliefs as 'stories we tell ourselves' can assist children to commence the work of loosening their hold. By emphasizing that thoughts are not the complete expression of the child, we are attempting to relieve them of the distress associated with identifying with the content of unhelpful or upsetting thoughts.

Observing myself

Much like cognitive defusion, when we are an observer to our thoughts, we can gain a little bit of space from them, loosening their grip on us. When combined with mindfulness, we can think about the idea of stepping outside of myself to notice my own thoughts, feelings or actions. Visualization techniques can be used to illustrate the concept of the observer. Some children like the idea of a Mini-Me sitting in the air, looking down on myself, noticing what I am doing. For Harry Potter fans, Dumbledore's Pensieve (Rowling 1999) is a wonderful representation of the observing self. The Pensieve is a magical tool that can syphon thoughts and memories from one's mind. These are poured into a basin where one can observe them. In this way, users of the Pensieve are better able to recognize patterns and themes in their thinking.

The following exercise involves a small character named Watchy the Owl (Wassner and Fleming 2015).

EXERCISE

The therapist draws a picture of a child standing on the ground and an owl perched above in a tree (Figure 8.3).

Figure 8.3

Therapist: Today we are going to do some work on noticing ourselves. Whenever we do things, a part of our brain watches what we do. We like to call this 'the watcher'. This part of our brain is a lot like Watchy the Owl. Watchy the Owl is always perched high in his favourite tree. He sits there all day and likes to watch what is happening around him. He is very curious and is really good at noticing what people are doing, how they are feeling and what they are thinking.

The watcher in our brain is like Watchy the Owl. Both like to sit above everything and just check out what is happening around them.

They don't get stressed out or worried about what they see; they just study what is going on with curiosity.

Here is a picture of a kid named Eden (therapist draws a small smiling child below Watchy). Notice on the top right-hand side that Watchy the Owl is doing his favourite thing – sitting and watching! Eden is having a good day; you can see that Eden is smiling. Write what thoughts you think Eden is having, and write beside Eden's body how you think he would be feeling. What do you think Watchy would see happening?

The child is encouraged to write any thoughts, feelings or behaviours noticed in Eden (e.g. relaxed, comfortable, low heartbeat, breathing slowly).

The exercise is then repeated with the child drawing a picture of himself. The child is invited to share a situation over the past few weeks when they felt scared or worried. Instead of an owl, the child can choose their preferred type of observer, representing their own 'watcher'. The child is invited to write down what their watcher would have observed when this happened.

The therapist and child can debrief by discussing how the watcher is able to provide the child with some space from the overwhelming sensations. A review of cognitive defusion and acceptance techniques will reinforce the idea that we can feel trapped and scared when difficult thoughts overwhelm us. By stepping out and noticing our thoughts as an outside observer, we can gain some breathing room and make clearer decisions.

CHESSBOARD METAPHOR: THINGS CHANGE, BUT I'M STILL ME

The chessboard metaphor (Hayes et al. 1999) is another ACT technique that encourages children to step out of their thoughts and observe what is happening in their mind. It can be explained in words, but it's easier to understand when shown on a real chessboard. It is also more engaging for children. The child is asked to name something positive about themselves and use a black chess piece to represent it. The chess piece is placed on the board. A child can then name something negative they feel about themselves, represented by a white piece, which is placed on the board in a way that pushes back the black piece. More self-perceptions are added via chess pieces, and this continues back and forth, noticing the struggle between the two sides. The more they fight, the more strongly the beliefs are held.

The child is then invited to step away from the board and imagine themselves as the chessboard itself. In this way, the child becomes an observer or a witness to the game but is not involved in the struggle. If we become chess pieces, we are drawn into the struggle. By stepping outside of the game and becoming a witness, we can drop the fight.

Therapist: If I were the chessboard, would it matter which side was winning or losing? Would it matter who is right or wrong?

By stepping outside the struggle, the child learns that the struggle is temporary and will pass.

The metaphor's application to the child will be critical during debrief. In particular, we want to recognize that some of the beliefs we hold about ourselves do not necessarily define who we are. They are temporary and changeable. We are instilling a sense of separation between our self as an observer and our self as a thought. You are the chessboard and you are a constant. The things we say or think can come and go, but I am still me. By recognizing the self as continuous, we can provide a stable sense of self – a safe place inside of me, a part of me that cannot be harmed.

TORCH ON THE BRAIN METAPHOR

The 'Torch on the Brain' metaphor can be used to help the child visualize themselves as an observer of a busy mind. In addition to illustrating the observing concept, the metaphor offers multiple points for discussion around cognitive defusion, mindfulness and acceptance. An animated version of Torch on the Brain is available for learners who respond better to video (Wassner 2021d). When utilizing a video version, it is suggested that the video be paused at various stages for debriefing and incorporating the child's own examples.

The therapist draws a rough semi-circle to represent the mind and then says:

Let's take a look at all of the incredible things that might be going on in your mind at the same time. Let's start with the five senses. All through the day, your mind notices stuff through *sight, smell, taste, touch* and *hearing*.

(The therapist draws ears, eyes, nose, mouth and hands within the mind to represent five senses awareness (Figure 8.4).)

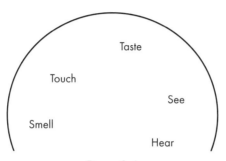

Figure 8.4

Sometimes we can notice it really strongly, like the delicious smell of popcorn at the movies as it wafts past our noses. We can also *choose* to notice something through our senses, even if it's not that strong. For example, right now, I can get your mind to notice the feeling of your foot inside your shoe. I just made your mind do that – no magic needed! How about trying to notice a sound you can hear? I bet you can hear lots of stuff. Maybe there is noise outside the room, like people talking, music or traffic. Maybe there are sounds inside the room, like the soft buzzing of an air conditioner. You might have noticed these things before I suggested it, or maybe not. Sometimes we can hear things without actually paying attention to them. But the sounds continue, and you can certainly hear them. Sometimes you pay the sounds lots of attention, and sometimes you barely notice them as they buzz along in the background.

Our minds also have a bunch of other stuff swirling around inside. We have thoughts coming and going through our minds all day, every day. We also have memories in there. We have some feelings as well as some ideas and urges.

The therapist adds various thoughts and emotions to the mind diagram (Figure 8.5). Where possible, the therapist should add some distressing thoughts and feelings that have been identified by the child during therapy.

Figure 8.5

Therapist: All of these things are rolling around in our minds all day, every day. Can you imagine how crazy life would be if we paid attention to all of these things at the same time? Pretty exhausting! So, the mind focuses on just a few things at a time. It's a little bit like having a torch pointed at your brain.

From here, the therapist can use an actual torch or simply point to different parts of the diagram as they are discussed (Figure 8.6).

Figure 8.6

Therapist: Remember when I told you to notice the feeling of your foot inside your shoe? I was getting your mind's torch to shine brightly on TOUCH. You were really noticing TOUCH in your foot at that moment. But did you notice that something else happened? All of the other stuff

WORKING WITH DIFFICULT THOUGHTS

in your mind got a bit quieter. Whenever the torch shines too brightly on one part of the brain, it's hard to notice the other things in there.

Sometimes the torch shines really brightly on a part of the brain that makes you feel pretty awful. Feelings can be particularly powerful like this. Have you ever noticed that when you feel really sad it's hard to think about anything else?

Did you know that our minds connect THOUGHTS and FEELINGS? Imagine that you have a strong angry feeling towards your brother. The torch would shine brightly on feeling angry, but it would also shine brightly on some thoughts, such as 'that is so unfair', 'he is so mean' and 'why does mum always take his side?'

How about when you're feeling worried? That torch would shine brightly on FEELING WORRIED and then brightly on WORRY THOUGHTS.

A therapist can add 'I can't do this', 'it's too hard' or 'I really don't want to go' inside the mind diagram.

Therapist: When the torch shines in this way, life can get pretty dreadful. The stronger the torch shines on these thoughts and feelings, the stronger they seem to get. I don't know about you, but when this happens to me, it ends up being a pretty horrible day, and I can't seem to get on with anything I'd really like to do.

But it doesn't have to be that way. We actually have the power to dim the torch so it's a little less bright, and share the light across other parts of the brain. In fact, we can choose to move the torch to something entirely different in our minds. Like one of the five senses. Let's try it. Can you notice three yellow objects right now? I'm guessing your mind's torch just moved over to SIGHT.

Using the five senses to notice different things doesn't get rid of the difficult thoughts or feelings, but it does make them quieter and easier to handle. We might still feel a bit worried, but if we take control of the torch, we can choose where our attention is most useful. Then we have a much better chance of getting on with our day and doing the stuff that's important.

There's nothing we can do to stop all of these uncomfortable thoughts and feelings from arriving in the first place. It's just what they do. They come and go all day long. But when WE decide where to shine the torch, we get to spend so much more time on the stuff that truly matters!

Bringing it all together

MINDTRAIN METAPHOR (WASSNER AND FLEMING 2015)

The mindtrain metaphor is a fun and playful technique that was created as an easy-to-use strategy incorporating noticing (mindfulness), cognitive defusion, acceptance and self as context. While the metaphor can be explained verbally, the impact is greater (and a lot more fun) when a toy train is set up.

Setup

- Toy train set.

- Train track.

- Toy platform or station somewhere along the track.

- A selection of the child's unhelpful thoughts and feelings written on small strips of paper. These are taped to the tops of the train carriages (one per carriage).

Therapist: I want you to imagine that you are standing here on the platform of the train station. In the distance, a train is approaching. Some of your thoughts and feelings are attached to the carriages of the train. As the train comes towards you, you can hear the rumbling of the train and the noise of the engine. You can feel the vibrations in your chest and the noise in your ears. As the train gets closer, your thoughts and feelings become louder and more uncomfortable.

Soon the train arrives at the platform. This is the loudest it can sound.

Some trains have many, many carriages and take a long time to come to a stop, while others only have a couple of carriages and arrive in a second flat. When the train is passing in front of you on that platform, it makes a lot of noise and can be really, really scary.

As you stand on the platform, you have a choice. It's up to you whether you choose to hop on the train or just stay on the platform and let it pass. You know that it will pass once it has picked up passengers. If you choose to stay on the platform, you will soon hear the noise of the engine disappearing into the distance and can appreciate the quiet that remains.

Did you know that all thoughts and feelings pass, just like a train? All thoughts and feelings, no matter how hard they are to handle, will pass if we let them. All thoughts are normal, and all feelings are normal. All thoughts pass, and all feelings pass. They never stay with us forever.

Pausing in this moment allows for a discussion around a time when the child chose to 'hop on the train'. The impact of staying on the train and feeling overwhelmed with our thoughts and feelings should be explored. Of note, the inner difficulties (feelings and thoughts) can become stronger and louder. Cognitive defusion or acceptance techniques can be revisited to help the child cope in these moments.

Therapist: Sometimes when things aren't going so well in life or when you feel particularly worried or afraid, it can help you to have some things to say to yourself to make you feel better, and these can help us to choose not to hop on the train and to let it pass by.

I don't really like this feeling, but I know it will pass.

This feels uncomfortable, but I can handle it.

This won't last forever; the train always passes.

I can choose to stay on the platform.

Summary

Acceptance and Commitment Therapy provides unique methods for navigating distressing thoughts. Psychoeducation around thoughts can assist children to recognize why difficult thoughts have shown up and assist them to unhook from them in a way that can reduce their unhelpful impact. The ACT principles of cognitive defusion, acceptance and self as context can be interwoven to enable children to notice, manage and defuse from cognitions that are interfering with their ability to get on with a meaningful life.

Chapter 9

ACT Applications to Obsessive Compulsive Disorder

Obsessive compulsive disorder (OCD) presents the ACT practitioner with some unique cognitive and behavioural hurdles, especially when working with children. OCD comprises two key components: obsessions and compulsions. Obsessions refer to unwanted or intrusive thoughts or urges that come into a person's mind repeatedly, usually causing distress and impacting the person's ability to get on with daily life. In OCD, obsessions originate in the mind and ask the sufferer to pay extreme attention to them. In earlier chapters, we learned how a threat response can narrow one's focus. In OCD, an obsessive thought is so uncomfortable that it is perceived to be threatening. The sufferer will focus heavily on that obsession, often to the exclusion of all else. This feels extremely distressing and they will typically do whatever they can to avoid those unwanted inner sensations. The quickest way to get rid of this discomfort is to engage in a behaviour related to the obsession. These are referred to as compulsions. When they occur repeatedly, we might refer to them as rituals.

A child could hold an obsessive thought around a need to touch their bedside lamp when their parents say 'goodnight' to them each evening. In order to avoid or get rid of this urge (touch the lamp) that originated from the distressing thought, the child engages in a compulsion. In this case, the child would touch the lamp in just the right way when their parents say 'goodnight'.

Engaging in a compulsion is a form of avoidance as the compulsive action avoids or puts a stop to the urge or thought (obsession). In Chapter 1, we explored the trouble that comes with excessive avoidance. In particular, when we avoid, the trouble comes back more powerfully.

In OCD, the obsession returns fairly quickly, leading the sufferer to repeat their compulsion to gain relief. Continually engaging in compulsions strengthens the OCD. In the above example, the mere action of touching the lamp provides immediate relief. This reinforces the very belief that the lamp must be touched every night to avoid the difficult inner experience (obsessive thought). Accordingly, the child's obsessive belief and related behaviour become rituals that seem to become stronger and stronger. As the OCD progresses, the need to get it 'just right' strengthens, leaving families feeling obliged to repeat the ritual over and over until the child is satisfied it is just right. Sometimes it is never enough. For many families, this has a notable impact on household functioning. In this case, parents may find that the child's bedtime obsession takes up so much time that they are unable to spend quality time with their other children.

Psychoeducation: How does OCD work?

When working with children, it can be beneficial to name OCD from the outset. Explaining to the child about how OCD functions can assist them to better create an action plan. Psychoeducation from an ACT framework involves two key components:

- Accept rather than struggle with the intrusive thought/urge/ obsession.

- Prevent oneself from engaging in those compulsions or rituals related to the obsessive thoughts.

ACT-based language discussed in previous chapters can be adapted to OCD by normalizing and accepting obsessions when they appear. Some key learnings may include the following:

- We have thousands of thoughts turning up every day...we can't stop these obsessive ones from showing up.

- Everyone has these types of thoughts.

- All thoughts are normal.

- All thoughts pass.

From here we can discuss when obsessions and compulsions become problematic. The child can be taught that the obsessive thought is not the problem. It becomes a problem when it takes up too much of our attention and pulls us away from what truly matters.

Therapist: The problem is not the thought. The problem is OCD getting hooked on them.

The following metaphor can assist children to notice when the OCD has hooked them in.

SWIMMING FISH METAPHOR

Imagine a group of fish swimming in the sea. There is a fisherman above, but most of the fish just keep swimming in the same direction without paying too much attention to the fisherman's hook. One fish suddenly gets hooked by the fisherman's line. How does the fish know when it is hooked? Well, it knows because it is no longer swimming where it had been planning to swim. It is fully focused on the hook and no longer able to continue on its intended path.

Children can be assisted to recognize that OCD pulls them away from their desired path or, more commonly, from doing whatever it is that they would rather be doing.

Therapist:

> When you get hooked on a thought, it can be hard to think of anything else. It kind of keeps you stuck.
>
> I don't mind if you have OCD, but it bothers me if it gets in the way of you doing what you want to do.
>
> A thought can show up and that's okay. When the mind starts to focus too heavily on it and pulls us away from what we'd rather be doing, then it becomes a problem.

It will also be important for the therapist to acknowledge the relief that compulsions can give.

Therapist:

Of course, you do it (wash your hands, touch the book etc.), I get why you do it. That sounds really scary. Doing it gives you relief.

From here we need to acknowledge that the urge to engage in a compulsion becomes stronger each time it is performed.

Therapist:

The problem is, every time you do it, it feeds your OCD. The more you give OCD, the more it takes.

OCD is hungry for certainty so it gets you to do things in one strict way. Once you do it, it's never enough. It makes you do it again and again and again.

This becomes a good opportunity to discuss what OCD has cost the child. Be careful not to judge as responses can be very personal. If a child struggles to name any costs, suggestions can be made (examples below).

Cost of OCD

- Time away from friends.
- Time away from my family.
- Makes me grumpy and mean to people I love.
- Stops me from sleeping.
- Stops me from starting my school work.
- Makes it hard for me to concentrate on my homework.
- Can't go on play equipment or rides anymore.
- Everyone gets mad at me for taking so long in the bathroom.

Debriefing the cost with compassion and acceptance will be important. The acknowledgment of the toll it has taken can increase willingness, setting the groundwork for managing compulsions. This is a crucial step before moving on to exposure.

Therapist:

That's annoying spending all that time on...

How much time would that take you each night?

Sounds like OCD is really interfering with life.

That sounds like a very exhausting evening.

What would life be like without it? What else could you be doing if you didn't have to spend your evenings doing that?

Some therapists like to refer to OCD as a bully that we need to stand up to. An ACT approach prefers to see OCD as a natural fear response that is stuck or confused. We do not need to hate the OCD but we can choose when we listen to it. When a child discusses their compulsions, a therapist can compassionately inquire about the following:

Do you want that or does your OCD want that?

It seems like OCD is telling you what to do.

What if you had more freedom to choose?

What can you do so next time this feeling has less power over you?

Imagine what else you could be doing with a whole extra hour every day.

Case example: Naming my OCD

Maddie was a 5-year-old girl who had been attending therapy to manage her anxiety. It quickly became apparent that Maddie was engaging in excessive checking behaviours, leading to constant reassurance seeking from her mother. Maddie would repeatedly ask her mother whether she had locked the windows at night, whether the outside gate was closed and whether the house was locked.

Maddie's mother attended a parent therapy session where OCD was explored and psychoeducation provided. Maddie's mother understood that her tendency to constantly reassure Maddie and comply with Maddie's checking requests only strengthened the OCD. She was committed to managing it quickly.

Maddie's mother returned to therapy the following week and introduced her homemade concept of 'Bossy Betty'. Bossy Betty had a habit of bossing Maddie around. She was constantly telling

Maddie what to do, saying things like 'check that lock', 'make sure your toys are safe', 'make sure Mum checked properly' and 'ask Mum again'. Maddie enjoyed the concept and took to it quickly. The next time Maddie asked her mother whether her toys were safe, Maddie's mother responded, 'Are you asking me to check that or is Bossy Betty asking?' By creating Betty, Maddie's mother had stumbled on to an excellent use of the ACT principles of cognitive defusion and self as context. Bossy Betty enabled Maddie to be an outsider looking in at her thoughts. It also provided her with some space from the troubling thoughts. Maddie immediately connected with the technique and was utilizing Bossy Betty in her own narrative within a few days. On one occasion, Maddie complained that 'Bossy Betty is ruining my day'. This was a great opportunity to explore how the checking was interfering with her ability to get on with her day. We could discuss how much time and energy Bossy Betty was taking. Maddie's Mum reported a significant decrease in reassurance seeking and checking behaviour.

Exposure response prevention

Having assisted children to recognize how OCD works, we commence our work on compulsions via exposure. Exposure is a commonly used strategy for treating OCD. The basic premise of exposure involves having the child resist the temptation to engage in a compulsion with a goal of reducing the power of the related obsession. Exposure response prevention (ERP) is a process in which the child is encouraged to face the discomfort associated with their obsessions or urges (exposure). Response prevention refers to the act of preventing oneself from engaging in the compulsion or obsession-related ritual. Cognitive behavioural therapy (CBT) has enjoyed enormous success on account of its evidence-based outcomes in relation to using exposure to treat OCD (Samantaray, Chaudhury and Singh 2018). As a result, most current practitioners have a good understanding of the CBT approach. It would therefore be useful to discuss some key conceptual differences between CBT and ACT regarding the way cognitions and exposure tasks are managed, to enhance understanding of the nuances in ACT.

A traditional CBT exposure-based exercise involves a therapist creating a hierarchy of fears to commence the work of systematic desensitization. Let us use the example of a child who is scared of germs. The therapist and child might create a list of activities in which the germ fear might show up, such as touching door handles, playing on play equipment and holding hands with friends. The child is then asked to rate each of these activities from most distressing to least distressing. This becomes the template for graded exposure. The child would be asked to face one of these activities at a time, starting with least distressing and moving towards most distressing. In order to gauge a child's readiness to be exposed, a therapist will often employ the use of a Subjective Unit of Distress Scale (SUDS). A SUDS score can also be sought after exposure for comparison. The child might agree to touch a door handle as part of their exposure treatment. They may rate their distress as 8/10 (high) before the exposure and 4/10 (low) after the exposure. Having completed the task successfully, a therapist could say, 'You see, it wasn't so bad, was it?', emphasizing the reduction in anxiety as noted in the SUDS score. Thanks to this reduction in fear level, the therapist would move on to the next feared activity in the hierarchy. Accordingly, fear reduction has become the goal.

An ACT approach hypothesizes that when our primary goal is fear reduction, struggle can reappear, resulting in a deepening of the fear in the long term. Rather than fear reduction, the measure of success in an ACT exposure would be a child's ability to better engage in the world in a way that is meaningful for them.

While the ACT approach to exposure might appear similar to CBT from a behavioural perspective (engaging in a feared behaviour), the way we select our exposure task differs. SUDS scores are not a usual feature of an ACT-based exposure exercise, nor are hierarchies of fear. Rather, choice of exposure task is based on the child's willingness to engage in the exposure and face their fear.

Techniques of cognitive defusion and acceptance create a context in which the young person can build their willingness to engage in an exposure task. Importantly, a review of values will assist the child to remember why facing their fear is so important. In so doing, we are assisting the child to move forward in a meaningful direction while being willing to carry their fear. Developing helpful thoughts to assist exposure will assist the willingness:

> It feels scary touching those monkey bars right now, but I'm going to do it because being able to play with my friends at lunchtime is important to me.

We are encouraging the young person to develop a willingness to learn new behavioural repertoire in the face of fear. Some might refer to the anxiety-related obsession as a sparring partner, a companion with whom we can learn to live. We do not have to like the anxiety that accompanies an obsession, but we are allowing its presence. Often, anxiety reduction is a welcome by-product of an exposure task but it is not the goal, for that could invite further struggle.

When the client is ready to engage in an exposure task, we begin by discussing the idea of expanding one's comfort zone. Children can be encouraged to explore and simply notice their outer experiences (what happens to their body) and inner experiences (thoughts, feelings and urges) when they move towards a fear. This incorporates the ACT concepts of self as context (being an outsider noticing myself) as well as mindfulness (pausing to notice my experience).

Noticing the fear during exposure is crucial as it reinforces the value of the task. This narrative builds towards an understanding that exposure will indeed be hard, but we are going to do it anyway in the service of a meaningful life.

Before asking a child to completely resist the temptation to engage in a compulsion, we can discuss playful ideas for engaging in the ritual a little differently. The child can be encouraged to engage in the ritual but in a different way, loosening the rigid hold of the obsession. Could the child delay their urge by one minute? Could the child engage in the ritual differently? To practise resisting urges, a therapist could blow bubbles and have the child resist the urge to pop them. Eventually, we want to expand the child's ability to resist the compulsion directly and in various contexts.

Case example: Values for OCD

Megan was a bright and friendly 10-year-old girl who was very much part of a friendship group at her school. Whenever the bell rang for recess or lunchtime, Megan experienced distressing obsessive thoughts regarding her desk tub in the classroom. She felt repeatedly compelled to check it was tidy. At first, she was able to do so quickly and her friends happily waited for her. Over time, the obsession grew stronger and her need to check and tidy grew more powerful. Soon she was needing to check and recheck so the entire ritual was taking a very long time. Before too long, friends started feeling annoyed and no longer waited for Megan. Megan desperately tried to complete her compulsions more quickly, but this led to more distress, and the urge to complete it more perfectly grew stronger and stronger.

Megan arrived at therapy with strong motivation to get on top of this problem. She recognized that her need to tidy her tub before play was taking a toll on her friendships. Through tears, she desperately expressed how much she wanted the intrusive thoughts to just stop. This gave an insight into Megan's values and paved the way for a treatment plan.

The cost of her OCD was first explored. Together, we discussed her values and discovered that being respectful and fun with her friends was really important to Megan. She recognized that tidying the desk tub was not only giving her shorter play time, but it was also taking away from her friends' play time. This was not the type of friend she wanted to be.

On further exploration, Megan disclosed that she noticed herself being horrible to her mother whenever she thought about her tub in the evenings. Megan also admitted that her sleep had deteriorated due to worrying about the issue at bedtime.

Sessions with Megan explored the fact that many of the things she cared about were at risk, so it was important to make a plan about resisting the urge to tidy her tub. At first, Megan felt unable to resist the urge completely but was willing to engage in a curiosity exercise that involved pausing and noticing the inner sensations (thoughts and feelings) she experienced when the bell for playtime rang.

Megan returned to therapy and reported that she did tidy her tub each day but she was also able to notice the sensations she was experiencing when the obsessions were very loud. She had noticed a racing heart, clammy hands and faster breathing. She also noticed various thoughts including 'just tidy it, it will only take a second', 'you need to tidy this, it'll be okay, just tidy it quickly' and 'I hope my friends don't mind'. Megan certainly did not like these thoughts and feelings but she expressed a willingness to experience these uncomfortable sensations and face her fear. Megan was still not ready to give up the tub tidying entirely but she was willing to do it differently. We talked about tidying in a different way or carrying out the process in a different order. Megan did so the following day and was slowly loosening the grip of the OCD hook.

A few weeks later, Megan said that she felt ready to resist the compulsion altogether; she would walk out of the class with her friends at recess without checking her tub. Values around friendships were reviewed and helpful cognitions were created to use during the exposure:

> I really want my desk tub to be neat. It's gonna be really uncomfortable not to check it but I'm willing to accept an unchecked tub at recess today and walk out the door with my friends because they are important to me.

Megan was additionally reminded to pause and notice any inner experiences (thoughts, feeling, urges) and outer experiences that might show up. We discussed the importance of noticing the fear during exposure and reminding herself why she was doing it. This was reinforced through the therapist expressing that Megan engaging in exposure was both scary and marvellous.

Megan succeeded in leaving the class without checking her tub on two separate days the following week. Megan's obsessions remained strong but she had commenced the work of loosening OCD's grip so she could move in a valued direction. Megan's path ahead would not be easy but with ongoing support and reminders of her values, she would slowly be spending more time doing the things that mattered to her.

Summary

OCD presents with unique challenges when it comes to working with children. Naming and recognizing how OCD works can assist parents and children to better understand their own OCD-related behaviour. The goal of an ACT intervention for OCD is spending more time engaging in things that matter to us. Obsessive thoughts and urges in OCD can take a highly debilitating toll on families. Treatment works on building a willingness to accept these obsessions while resisting the temptation to engage in the obsession-related compulsion.

Chapter 10

Application to Neurodivergent Populations

Neurodiversity is a term used to describe differences in individual brain function. It is regarded as a normal variation in the human population (Singer 2017). In essence, neurodivergent (ND) individuals perceive and experience the world differently to the majority of people, termed neuro-typicals (NTs). Neurodivergence is most commonly associated with, although not limited to, autism, challenges with executive function and attention, sensory processing difficulties and learning difficulties. This chapter will focus on autism and attention deficit hyperactivity disorder (ADHD). It is estimated that 50–70 per cent of autistic individuals also present with co-occurring ADHD (Hours, Recasens and Baleyte 2022), so it is essential to consider the key features of both when working with neurodivergent populations.

With unconditional compassion-focused acceptance at the very core of ACT principles, it is no surprise that practitioners have enjoyed great success when applying strategies to neurodivergent children. The acceptance canvas provides a wonderful start for building rapport thanks to its emphasis on social safety in the therapy room, the love of diversity and the tendency for some quirky strategies.

There are three key features common to neurodivergent children that require special consideration when applying ACT-based strategies:

1. *Perception and response* Neurodivergent people perceive and experience the world differently to NTs. They may not respond to explicit teaching of skills in the way other children might.

2. *Rigidity* Psychological flexibility is a central ACT goal, so intervention necessarily focuses on a willingness to do things differently.

Many ND individuals, particularly those on the autism spectrum, approach life with great rigidity. Rigidity can feel safe in an unpredictable world that has been designed for NTs.

3. *Social rejection* Evolutionarily, humans strongly desire to fit in and to feel as though we belong to a tribe or social group. Because so many autistic individuals need alone time to regulate, many NTs can mistake this as an overall preference for being alone at all times or having no desire to belong with others. This is far from true. Autistic individuals have a strong need to belong and feel socially safe. Unfortunately, many describe a long history of social rejection, impacting their threat system and capacity for new skill building. Children with impulsive/hyperactive ADHD often experience rejection for other reasons. They may be considered too loud, annoying or 'in your face' by their peers.

Neurodiversity and acceptance

The neurodiversity paradigm encourages NDs to recognize and embrace their differences. Individuals are guided to be their true selves. This can be tremendously challenging within the child's backdrop of feeling different and a history of social rejection. Psychoeducation around the concept of neurodiversity can assist children to accept and even welcome their differences.

Therapist: Have you heard of neurodiversity? I think it's something you'd be really interested in. The word 'neuro' means nerves, but we really use it to describe the brain. Most human brains are wired in a fairly similar way. That means most people notice things and respond to them in much the same way. We call these people 'neurotypicals'. Then we have those people who notice and respond to the world a bit differently. We call them 'neurodivergent'. The five senses are a great example of this. Have you ever noticed that some people can smell things more powerfully than everyone else? Or maybe they get bothered by things such as tags on their clothes? That's because those people are neuro-divergent and their senses (smell and touch) are super strong for them. Some neurodivergent kids have the opposite. They don't notice stuff that everyone else does. I know a kid who doesn't notice when it's cold and he walks around in shorts all winter. When people notice stuff in a different way to most people, it doesn't mean they're right or wrong; they're just different, or neurodivergent.

NEURODIVERSITY: THEATRE METAPHOR

Therapist: Imagine that you and Mum decide to go on a trip to the theatre. You both enjoy the show and afterwards go to a restaurant to enjoy a pancake together where you discuss the show. Mum starts talking about characters and all the things that were happening in the storyline. You might talk about the lighting or the stage set. It doesn't mean one of you got the show wrong. All it means is that your minds noticed different aspects of it.

Finding my strengths, finding my tribe

When a young person understands and accepts their neurodivergence, they become better able to engage in self-compassion and discuss their difference positively. This allows them to drop the struggle with 'trying to be normal' and celebrate their strengths. Children can be encouraged to find like-minded peers with similar interests. When this is achieved, most neurodivergent children will immediately experience an enhanced sense of social safety, leading to a reduction in anxiety and an increase in self-esteem. Only then does flexibility become accessible. A basic internet search will yield numerous books and websites describing strengths and famous people associated with neurodiversity. Many autistic children are already excelling in engineering, creativity and artistic talents, to name a few. In terms of day-to-day traits, they may be exhibiting outstanding attention to detail or may be exceptionally honest and loyal. Researching and celebrating these strengths will remain paramount throughout the lifespan and should be encouraged during therapy sessions in an ongoing way.

When children do not understand and celebrate neurodiversity, they can experience serious self-esteem issues. They may view themselves as weird and feel distressed that they are unable to be like everybody else. 'Masking' is a term that describes when autistic children focus heavily on trying to appear neurotypical for the purpose of appeasing their peers and fitting in. They may resist urges or try overly hard to fit in. Masking, however, leads to extreme exhaustion and behavioural difficulties and/ or mental health problems often follow.

Self-acceptance is a crucial feature of anxiety reduction in autistic children. Encouraging them to love their difference, embrace their special interests and develop skills in an area of strength can truly move them in the direction of self-acceptance. Once they are able to simply like themselves more and spend less time masking, we see a reduction in anxiety. For some, this additionally opens up their capacity to find like-minded peers, a sense of community and a sense of belonging. This must be prioritized in therapy, for without a sense of social safeness, the child is far less likely to be able to engage in the important work of psychological flexibility.

I recall working with a young autistic boy who loved dogs. He told me that he would take his dog Milo to the dog park every afternoon. The moment he removed his leash, Milo would instantly run into the middle of the pack of dogs and start playing with them joyfully. The boy was amazed at how Milo ran into the pack, no qualms, and just knew what to do. He commented that in the playground at school, he felt like a cat at the dog park. He just didn't know how to approach, play or chat with the other kids. It was much akin to being in a foreign land. This sense of being a foreigner is common for autistic individuals trying to navigate an NT world. It can be frustrating and feel like a constant struggle. The Japan metaphor was created to help children find meaning and connection in a foreign context. Many autistic children hold Japan as a special interest, hence its selection for the metaphor.

JAPAN METAPHOR

Therapist: I'd like you to imagine that you decide to move to Japan. You are interested in so many things about Japan including the lifestyle, the technology, the train systems and the customs. You spend months learning the language, reading up about customs and learning about the food. You arrive in Japan and find your way around pretty well, enjoying many of the things you had researched. There are times, however, when you make mistakes. You might misunderstand a Japanese custom and carry it out incorrectly. Maybe you bow too low or you don't bow low enough to someone you have met. You would probably make some language mistakes too and you realize that Japanese will never be as fluent as your English.

Life in Japan will never feel as natural and easy-going as it might in a country that you're more used to. You think about ways to make life more workable despite these obstacles. You find ways to focus on the things you love. Eventually, you meet other English speakers living in Japan and you are able to spend relaxed time chatting to them. You also meet some Japanese people who are fascinated by Western culture and want to learn English. They love your difference and are keen to enjoy your company. Over time, you find a way to have a meaningful life in a place that can, at times, be confusing.

This metaphor encourages young people to accept the difficulties that accompany the feeling of being different or constantly misunderstood. The metaphor emphasizes the value in finding social connection and meaning, despite these obstacles.

Sensory processing differences

Sensory processing differences are extremely common among ND individuals. When sensitivity is high, flexibility is low, so a thorough understanding of a child's sensory needs is crucial before embarking on any work around psychological flexibility. Occupational therapists are trained to complete comprehensive sensory profiles and provide recommendations. Other professionals who work with autism should ensure they, too, have insight into a child's sensory profile, as it can impact functioning across multiple domains in a most significant way. The following section aims to assist therapists to understand and accommodate a neurodivergent child's sensory needs. You may choose to consult an occupational therapist for more in-depth understanding.

Building a sensory profile

The child-friendly explanation of neurodiversity (above) makes reference to our five senses for simplicity, even though eight senses are widely recognized. Knowledge of all eight senses will assist therapists to create a detailed sensory profile:

- visual

- auditory

- olfactory (smell)

- gustatory (taste)

- tactile

- vestibular (balance)

- proprioception (knowing where my body is in space)

- interoception (ability to identify, understand and respond to inner body states, e.g. hunger, temperature).

The sensory profile must be taken into account before trying to assist young people to be relaxed so they can be willing and ready to learn the skills of psychological flexibility.

A child with an over-responsive sensory system notices their sensory experiences in more extreme ways. This may include finding noises too loud, touch too intense or smells too strong. When these experiences are perceived, it is genuinely painful and can overwhelm the individual, impacting their ability to remain relaxed, to learn or simply to get on with their day. If you are neurotypical, I'd like you to think about how hard it would be to get on with your daily tasks while a loud ringing sound is constantly present. Fairly innocuous stimuli, such as a subtle smell, can feel this intense and disturbing for those who are over-responsive to sensory input.

Some individuals are under-responsive to sensory stimuli. These individuals seek out sensory input to feel more regulated. These children might need to run, fidget or climb and can be very obvious in those with hyperactive/impulsive ADHD. Other sensory-seeking behaviours may include pacing, pen-flicking or rocking. 'Stimming' is defined as repetitive or unusual movements or noises such flapping or spinning. Stimming assists many autistic children to self-soothe or regulate. It enables them to manage overwhelming emotions and feel more relaxed. Autistic people often comment that they are being their authentic selves when they are allowed to engage in any form of sensory seeking/ soothing including stimming. Importantly, allowing a young person to engage in their sensory-seeking behaviour enhances relaxation, so in the therapy room they are ready to learn. Young people in the therapy room should know from the outset that any form of sensory seeking is welcome. When working with parents, it is recommended that parents freely allow sensory-seeking and self-soothing behaviour at home, to maximize the chance of their child feeling regulated more often.

Sensory-seeking behaviour can sometimes be considered inappropriate in neurotypical settings. Parents are often concerned that sensory-seeking behaviours make their child a target for ridicule. This may be true, and many children are painfully aware of this, causing them to 'hold it in' at school. This can often result in the child requiring more opportunities to engage in sensory-seeking behaviour after school. When this is denied, behavioural outbursts can follow. For older children, it may be necessary to have an honest discussion about the likely responses of others when engaging in sensory-seeking behaviour in public and assist the child to decide whether masking these urges is worthwhile temporarily. Of course, it depends on the circumstances and the supports around the child at the time. If a child has decided that masking is worthwhile in a particular context, it will be important to recognize that doing so will be costly from a regulation perspective, and the child should be encouraged to engage in rest and self-care for the remainder of the day. The same can be said for eye contact. People who understand neurodiversity would not demand eye contact but there may be circumstances in which it does need to be made, such as when giving a speech or attending an interview when older.

Therapist: I realize there are times when you need to do uncomfortable stuff like giving eye contact at school. When you're in this room with me, you are under no obligation to give me eye contact because my preference is that you're comfortable and that your brain is wide and open to whatever it is that we're going to do today.

Many children on the autism spectrum can be under-responsive in some circumstances and over-responsive in others. Regardless of the direction of their sensory needs, children will experience difficulties relaxing and engaging in skill building when their sensory needs are not met. Therapists should take care in establishing a clear sensory profile of the child to ensure their sensory needs are accounted for during therapy sessions.

Sensory-friendly therapy room

Chapter 2 provides many examples of sensory-friendly rooms including various seating choices and fidget toys. It is strongly suggested that they be revisited and implemented, when preparing the therapy room for an ND child. These will be especially important for those children who are sensory seeking. They require sensory input to feel safe, regulated and ready to engage. Children should be allowed to move about the room freely and have objects on offer for touching and fidgeting. The therapist should explicitly discuss sensory-seeking behaviours with the child, emphasize knowledge of the benefits and ensure the child feels completely comfortable engaging in sensory-seeking behaviour in the therapy room at all times.

Discomfort with eye contact is a well-recognized feature of autism, and some social skills programmes try to teach or force young people to practise it. When an autistic person feels safe and heard, they will often say that they find eye contact too intense and that it reduces their ability to focus on what the speaker is saying. For the purposes of the therapy room, a place of safety and learning, it is recommended that autistic children are not forced to provide eye contact.

A therapist can also ask a child about their sensory needs explicitly.

- Are you the kind of kid that likes it to be warm or cold? Why don't you decide whether I put on the air-conditioning today.

- Does it smell okay for you in here or would you like me to open the window?

By setting up a room that is sensory-friendly and making mention of it, you are sending an implicit message that you acknowledge and understand their sensitive needs. Once this is established, we can commence the work of skill building via psychological flexibility.

Social anxiety

Social anxiety is extremely common among ND individuals. ND traits and behaviours can be perceived as inappropriate, annoying or weird by NTs, frequently resulting in the ND individual being bullied either explicitly or via exclusion. It is therefore no surprise that many ND individuals experience very high rates of social distress.

Recall that when we feel threatened socially, our capacity to engage in pro-social behaviour is reduced. This becomes a circular problem, with ND children becoming further excluded and feeling more rejected, which in turn reduces their capacity for learning. Social skills training becomes a delicate proposition.

Explicit social skills training

Explicit social skills training for ND children, such as worksheets or social skills groups, often require the young person to learn how to do things to make them appear more neurotypical. We know, however, that when ND children try too hard to appease their neurotypical peers, significant stress can result, due to their reduced ability to execute these skills naturally. That being said, many of these skills can be very important and will certainly assist the child in various contexts. There are many resources available for teaching explicit social skills to neurodivergent children but an in-depth review is outside of the scope of this book. From an ACT perspective, when a therapist chooses to engage in explicit social skills training with an autistic child, it must be presented within a compassionate acceptance framework that makes clear reference to the *context* in which these skills may be used.

Therapist: Do you remember when we talked about the difference between neurotypical and neurodivergent kids? We were discussing how most kids are neurotypical and they seem to notice and react to the world in pretty much the same way as one another. Then there are the neurodivergent kids, like you. Your mind notices different stuff and might react in a different way. That's why sometimes you look at typical kids and can't understand how they can get so excited about certain things, like a famous footballer. You hate football! Typical kids might look at you and have no idea how you can be so interested in buildings.

The differences are not just about our interests, though; it's also how we approach the world. It's almost like you speak two different languages. The problem for you is that most people are neurotypical, so they're all speaking the same 'language' and it's easier for them to understand one another. You might not get half the stuff they do or say. To make life easier for you, it would be helpful for you to learn a bit about how they do things. We can learn things about how neurotypicals do group work, or have conversations when they meet new people.

I'm not going to teach you these skills because there's something wrong with how you do it now; it will just make life easier for you when you're around neurotypicals.

Some children will comment that it seems unfair that they need to learn how to do things the neurotypical way because most neurotypicals don't bother to learn about neurodiversity. This is indeed true and sad. Reassure the child that there are many people who value neurodivergent kids and make the effort to learn their language, including parents, friends, teachers and therapists. Let's also remember that ND individuals have a natural way of communicating with one another, affectionately termed 'our neurokin'. Reinforcing earlier learnings about connecting with like-minded peers can be helpful at this point.

Many ND children know social rules but can experience difficulties putting them into real-life situations. It is the nuances in interaction that often lead to misunderstandings. Implicit social skills through an ACT lens provide much scope for assisting children to better manage social interactions.

Implicit social skills training

For many bright ND children, intelligence is highly valued. They often believe they are 'right' and may resist admitting their error or accepting help when things unravel socially. For these children, explicit social skills training can be downright offensive.

Implicit social skills training is very ACT compatible. Its compassionate lens focuses on incidental mindfulness (noticing) and workability. For younger children, skills of turn taking, agenda completion, sharing and good sportsmanship can be achieved very successfully via games during therapy sessions. Chapter 2 details multiple examples of these types of games with tips for encompassing skill building. These strategies are highly applicable to ND children and are encouraged to be revisited. They make for an enjoyable therapy session while subtly building important social skills.

For older children, more nuanced skills need to be taught, particularly when they deny their role when social problems emerge. One useful method is to teach the skill while referring to other children. This is often better achieved by coaching parents rather than teaching in the therapy room, as the child can typically see through the therapist's intention.

Parents can be coached to make incidental social comments. For example, a parent might be driving their two kids home from school, the older being autistic and the younger neurotypical. The autistic child may be unwilling to engage in conversation about their day at school, particularly the social aspects. Their sibling might offer more discussion. When this happens, the parent can respond to the neurotypical child in a way that provides their autistic child (who is no doubt listening) with implicit messaging.

Example 1:

NT sibling: Today Lily fell over in the playground. She was crying but none of her friends were there so I took her to the nurse.

Mother: That was very kind of you to notice she needed help and to take her. She must like you. I bet she would help you next time you need something.

Example 2:

NT sibling: I played with someone different today. I discovered Olivia also loves animals; we had so much fun.

Mother: It's a great idea to try different friends and notice whose company you seem to enjoy.

Within the therapy room, general discussion about other children can also assist. For those who are involved in team sports, one could assist the child to recognize the distinction between a skilled player and a player who shows good sportsmanship.

Therapist: Let's write down some of the skills you need to be good at basketball.

The skills are recorded under two columns as shown below:

Column A Scoring baskets	Column B Team stuff
Good at baskets	Passes
Fast	Encourages team mates
Good ball handling	Helps people when they fall
Good defence	Congratulates the other team
Strong	Good loser

Now let's write down the names of all the boys in your basketball team.

The therapist can then ask the child to name the person who is the best player in his team for each of the columns. Gentle discussion around further characteristics of each child can be obtained, leading to a discussion of the type of friend they are and how they are generally treated by others.

Therapist: So, Zac is the best at column B. Does he have many friends? Do the kids like him?

What's Zac like when he's not playing basketball?

There are many other skills that can be taught incidentally. This requires the therapist to be keenly attuned to presenting issues and what is brought to the therapy room on any given day. I recall working with an 8-year-old boy some years ago. He arrived to his first appointment with his parents and immediately started swearing excessively. His parents were extremely embarrassed and repeatedly asked him to stop. There was a long history of externalizing behavioural problems at both home and school with consequences yielding negligible behavioural changes. It was clear that the child experienced minimal positive feedback from adults. After all, there were so few opportunities for praise. I decided to delay any attempts to manage behaviour such as swearing and to focus on self-concept.

Sessions progressed via game playing, and although the swearing continued, the child slowly engaged more and more appropriately in sessions. He was improving in his ability to turn take, and incidences of cheating were reducing. After several weeks, we were sitting on the floor, playing a game of cards. There had been loud noises outside the clinic from the building site next door, but on this occasion, it was particularly disruptive. In line with implicit skill development, I used the opportunity to explore his responses.

Me: That construction work is driving me crazy. They are getting louder and louder.

The child put his cards down, stood up and said, 'That's okay, I'll go downstairs now and tell them to f*** off.'

I had no intention of reprimanding the coarse language. Rather, I was presented with a golden opportunity to build his self-concept.

Me: Thanks, buddy, that's really kind of you to offer to do that for me. But no, I reckon that'd just make things worse. Thanks for wanting to help me, though.

When engaging in social skills training, it can be tempting to correct every inappropriate behaviour as it arises. By stepping out of the situation, recognizing the context and creating goals that reflect what is possible for the child, one can pace skill building at an achievable level.

Values

Abstract concepts such as values are often poorly understood by autistic children. In order to gain a true appreciation of their values, one may need to modify questioning so it becomes more concrete in nature. In Chapter 6, we explored ideas for eliciting values with concrete thinkers via asking the following:

- What do you really care about?

- What do you love doing?

- What do you really want?

The nature of these questions may yield concrete responses from some autistic children such as:

- To be normal.

- I'd like to do homeschooling.

- I want kids to stop leaving me out.

- I want to feel less anxious/lonely/angry.

- I want my brain to be normal.

- I just want people to leave me alone.

- I want to be an only child.

- I want to have more friends.

- I just want to be allowed to draw all day.

Although these responses are inflexible and not values at all, they are a great start. They provide clear insight into what is bothering the child. The clinician will take careful note of these comments and translate them into values. For example:

- I want to make friends who accept the real me.

- When I'm older, I want a job that I love.

- I want to be a respected member of my family.

- I want to be a kind and loyal friend.

- I want to spend time doing the things that I love.

- I want to recognize my strengths and use them.

When a therapist transforms the child's comments in this way, they are creating a sense of hope.

Therapist: This is stuff we can work on!

Once we have established a set of values, we can use them to navigate problems as they are presented in the therapy room in much the same way as discussed in Chapter 6.

Case example: Examining workability

Poor hygiene is an issue that is common among autistic people. Many parents raise concerns about their child's reluctance to shower, brush their teeth or brush their hair. The following example illustrates the utility of values with a shower-resistant 12-year-old autistic female.

Twelve-year-old Sophie had just entered secondary school. She had hated primary school, where she struggled socially and experienced frequent bullying. Sophie described loving her new school and had made great friends with whom she felt she could be her true self. Sophie was the happiest I had ever seen her.

Sophie's mother joined our therapy session to discuss her concerns about Sophie's body odour. She had commenced puberty and was reluctant to shower or use deodorant. Her mother had spent many years consoling Sophie through episodes of social rejection. She was understandably concerned that Sophie's new friends would soon reject her, due to her body odour. Sophie's mother spoke openly to Sophie about these concerns but Sophie's response was defensive. She truly disliked showering and was easily irritated by anything her mother suggested.

Upon discussion, it became instantly apparent that Sophie's perception of the problem differed markedly to that of her mother. The pair had a long history of battling over shower time. Sophie saw this situation as a mere extension of a familiar battle and she was not at all bothered about her smell. Sophie also proudly commented that her new friends like her for who she is and she did not believe they would judge her if she smelt.

While it was pleasing to see the vast improvement in Sophie's self-esteem and social connections, there was a reality behind the hygiene problem.

I had known Sophie for a while and had already established a good relationship with her, enabling me to suggest the following: 'Your new friends sound awesome. Tell me about the type of friend you would like to be for them.'

From here, we discussed ideas around respectful friendships, including how we present our bodies. I reminded Sophie of her tactile sensitivity and how she had to cut all of the tags out of her clothes. Sophie was then gently reminded about the other senses, particularly smell. We discussed the fact that some of her friends might be sensitive to smell and what it would be like for them to sit in a friendship group where there was an unpleasant odour.

Sophie was never going to enjoy showering. She found it uncomfortable and boring. After exploring her values (being a respectful friend), she became willing to wash more regularly.

Avoidance

Levels of internal distress can be extremely high for ND individuals during social situations, so encouraging the child to connect with their values and march through difficulty might not be enough to yield meaningful behaviour change. Progress may be slow and psychoeducation around avoidance is often a helpful start. Avoidance behaviour might allow for relief in the short term but typically creates greater problems in the long term. The social distress commonly experienced by autistic individuals can lead to extreme avoidance. The following questions can be used to elicit some of the child's avoidance behaviours.

Therapist:

- When you're feeling really awful, what do you do?

- If I was in your house/classroom, what would I notice about you if you were having a bad day? What would I see you doing?

Common avoidance behaviours in autistic children

- Withdrawing to a quiet place where they can be alone.

- Physically acting out – hitting, screaming, swearing, slamming doors.

- Hiding under desks.

- Online gaming.

- Giving up.

- Running away.

- Reading.

- YouTube.

- Eating.

- Breaking toys.

- Fantasy – books, movies, video games, costumes.

Therapists should approach the list gently and without judgement. First, we compassionately express our understanding:

- I can understand why you yelled at your sister. It was very stressful.

- No wonder you went into your room and slammed the door. It sounds like you really needed to be alone that day.

- Having some quiet time with your book certainly sounds like a much more peaceful option.

Next, we need to acknowledge the positive gains acquired from some of these avoidance strategies. Gaming, for example, is extremely common and an issue frequently raised by parents. Online gaming can provide children with a structure for the day. It can provide a sense of purpose and avoids the discomfort of unpredictability. Many children experience a great sense of achievement through gaming and may even be recognized for their skill by their peers. This is a sense of success that they may not find at school or in the playground. Fantasy can provide a sense of escaping and being someone else. Children love to build their own world and become a different character. They can gain great satisfaction and pride out of this. Behavioural avoidance around school work can benefit a child in the short term as it may provide the relief that 'nobody will find out I can't do it'.

For behaviours that are more externalizing in nature, such as swearing or yelling, we can acknowledge the release component.

- Sometimes when we're stressed, we do things to help us cope.

- When we find ourselves in a situation that makes us angry, yelling can make us feel better in that moment. It gives a sense of relief.

Once established, it will be important to explore the long-term outcomes of the unworkable behaviour.

Example from Mitch (11-year-old autistic male)

Mitch: Our family got a new iPad and all day long I had been begging Mum to have a turn on it. Mum kept saying no screens until the afternoon. At 1 o'clock, I saw my sister on the iPad. I couldn't believe Mum let her have it first. I'm the one who loves technology and I had been asking all day. Mum always favours Steph; it was so unfair. Steph poked her tongue out at me so I pushed her. Then I was the one who got in trouble. Mum always takes Steph's side.

A story such as this provides much scope for intervention. Careful questioning can assist Mitch to recognize where things went wrong.

Therapist: So, Steph poked her tongue out at you? That must have felt like she was really teasing you, especially since she had the iPad. But you were the one who ended up in trouble. How did that happen?

From here, we can explore how an action such as pushing his sister provided relief. It gave him a short burst of relief as he felt justice was being served. Steph would have been upset when pushed, so, for a brief moment, Mitch was able to avoid the feeling that Steph was winning. The push, however, gave some unwelcome consequences very quickly, including losing all screen privileges for the rest of the weekend.

By acknowledging the hurt Mitch felt and helping him to connect his behaviour (pushing) with a feeling he wanted to avoid (injustice), Mitch was able to commence the early stages of noticing the link between avoidance of inner difficulty and unworkable behaviour. As these skills developed, Mitch would become increasingly more competent at recognizing the workability of his behaviours.

When is a behaviour defined as avoidance?

Many of the avoidance behaviours listed above comprise some import-ant regulating strategies of ND children. Fantasy and gaming, for example, can provide the necessary quiet downtime that they need to regulate. Clarification around when a behaviour becomes problematic can be useful. An exploration around the *intention* behind a behaviour becomes paramount:

Therapist: Gaming can help us feel much better than we would feel sitting at our desk for homework. When we game to avoid something difficult, it can cause bigger problems in the long term. The homework doesn't do itself and we still have to face school the next day. That doesn't mean gaming is always bad. Sometimes it's useful to think about WHY we are doing it. If we are gaming because we've nailed a hard task and want some chill time, then gaming can be a great idea. But we have to be careful when we're using it to avoid unpleasant things like unwanted conversations with family members or avoiding school work. Even if you still want to game, it's important to ask yourself whether you're doing it to avoid something or just doing something positive for yourself.

Working with difficult thoughts and feelings

Managing difficult inner experiences, such as thoughts and feelings, comprises an important component of any ACT intervention. We have already explored ideas for working with difficult thoughts and feelings. The most notable challenge in using these with ND children is around identifying which thoughts and feelings require attention. Methods of cognitive defusion, self as context and acceptance are explored in detail in Chapter 8 and can be easily adapted to the cognitions and feelings described below, once they have been identified.

With neurotypical children, a therapist will tend to ask the young person what those experiences might be. Autistic children can feel unsure or even stressed when asked to describe their thoughts and feelings. Some autistic children have poor interoception and have little idea about these inner sensations in the first place. Many neurodivergent children have oftentimes been told that their feelings or thoughts are wrong or inappropriate, so they are reluctant to provide answers. Some are overly concerned about what others think and have a long history of masking; they fear being told that they are wrong or perhaps fear they will even be in trouble for answering incorrectly. In an attempt to please the inquirer or simply get it over with, many ND children will provide a plausible answer; a narrative to their situation that will satisfy the therapist.

In order to acquire more authentic responses from a neurodivergent child in therapy, a therapist should emphasize that there are no right or wrong answers. Children can be guided to notice physiological sensations but cognitions can be harder. Given the tendency for autistic children to provide honest answers when questioned directly, it can be helpful to suggest possible thoughts and ask them whether that happens for them.

Therapist: I once chatted to a kid about your age who also hated going to school in the morning. He told me that he kept worrying that he would get in trouble for something, even though he tried hard to do the right thing. Is that something your mind tells you?

In order to successfully suggest relevant experiences when eliciting difficult thoughts and feelings, therapists should ensure they are knowledgeable about themes common to neurodiversity. Below are examples of themes that are common to many neurodivergent children, resulting in strong inner experiences.

Social rejection

Recognizing and managing the cognitions that contribute to social anxiety will be very important. It cannot be assumed that cognitions that show up for neurotypicals with social anxiety are the same for autistic individuals. Social anxiety is defined as a fear of being negatively evaluated by other people (American Psychiatric Association 2013). It can occur in autistic and non-autistic populations but the nature of the anxiety can differ. Neurotypical social anxiety tends to focus on how I am presenting to others: Do I look good enough? Am I smart enough? When exploring the cognitions around social anxiety in autistic children, the focus is often more around 'getting it right'. They tend to worry more about stuffing things up or getting in trouble. This fear likely originates from previous experiences in which they have interpreted the world in a manner that is not accepted by neurotypicals and have found themselves reprimanded for reasons they do not comprehend. Many autistic children attend school with a strong desire to please teachers, but find themselves in trouble for reasons they cannot understand. These children arrive at school each day, nervous about being told off.

- Even when I tried to be a 'good girl' and behave as appropriate or expected, I was forever getting things wrong.

I recall working with a 12-year-old boy who had just returned from a meeting with his learning support teacher. Together they had devised a plan to assist him when he cannot understand the school work. The teacher was warm and kind and believed they had worked on the plan collaboratively. Upon chatting to the boy, he told me that he did not like the plan and could not envisage himself carrying it out successfully.

When I asked why he agreed to the plan earlier that day, he said, 'I thought I would get in trouble if I said I wanted to do it differently.'

On another occasion, I was working with an autistic 10-year-old boy with high levels of impulsive ADHD, who had been suspended from school that week. He had attended meetings at the school with his parents and had been made to complete a reflection worksheet about his behaviour, which the school determined was 'unsatisfactory'. During therapy, I asked what had happened the day he was suspended. It was clear from his narrative that he knew of the incident to which people were referring, but did not understand why he had been suspended.

Fear of rejection is another common cognition that requires addressing. When this fear becomes extreme, unhelpful behaviours often follow. For some, the desire to make social connection is so strong that young people might suffocate their friends. Autistic children may be less able to read the social cues around not being wanted. Eventually, the suffocated friend may withdraw. At the other extreme, fear of rejection can lead to a young person withdrawing entirely from social situations. An important inner struggle experienced by autistic children is around their sense of identity, so this needs to be explored carefully in the context of their social world and their ability to be their authentic selves.

While recognizing the nature of a child's social anxiety will be important, it is equally important to listen to the child's needs within different contexts. At times, withdrawing from socializing at lunchtime can be a positive for autistic children. Class time can be overwhelming, so the child may need a genuine break from their peers. Recharging alone at lunchtime is sometimes what is needed. Well-meaning school staff can become overly anxious about children sitting alone at lunchtime. I once worked with an 8-year-old girl who genuinely needed a social break at lunchtime but continued to play with a group of girls, even though she felt quite bored and annoyed in their company. She would have much preferred reading in the library. When I asked her why she did that, she told me she thought it was compulsory to play with others at lunchtime. This belief had originated from the many well-meaning adults who had been attempting to engineer friendships. By identifying this belief, we were able to guide parents and teachers to take the pressure off lunchtime and encourage social connections at other times such as weekends. Once this was clarified, she was able to read her book quietly at lunchtime and return to her classroom refreshed and better able to engage in the afternoon class both academically and socially. She was also much better regulated when she arrived home in the afternoon.

Perfectionism

Many ND children are extremely bright and struggle cognitively when they are unable to consistently uphold their standards. Therapists should consider those children who are bright but may be under-achieving in class. Common cognitions may include 'I'm dumb', 'this is too hard', 'I'm an idiot' and 'I'll never get a job'. In these circumstances, children may quickly avoid school work, so issues of procrastination and persistence should be explored. Persistence can be especially problematic for bright kids. In the early days of learning, many could complete tasks with ease. They move through school, however, and over time tasks become more difficult. Many bright kids have never had to practise putting effort and persistence into place, causing them to feel extremely stuck. Cognitions around perfectionism should therefore be explored thoroughly.

The double empathy problem

There is a common misconception that young people on the autism spectrum lack empathy. The double empathy problem posits that when people with very different experiences of the world interact with one another, they will struggle to empathize with each other. Hence, neurotypical people commonly perceive autistic responses as lacking in empathy. We know that neurodivergent people can be extremely empathetic, but it is shown differently. Many autistic individuals will report feeling or taking on another's emotions. An autistic child might come home and perceive that their mother is sad. That child then becomes sad themselves. This is a type of extreme empathy that many neurotypical people would neither experience nor comprehend.

This breakdown in understanding between neurotypical and neurodivergent individuals can cause great distress and is a suggested area for exploration when eliciting cognitions, particularly around empathy.

Strong sense of justice

It is recognized that children on the autism spectrum often have a very strong sense of justice. When they believe that something has been done unfairly, particularly to them, they can experience very strong emotions and difficulties unhooking from related cognitions. Their threat system is strongly activated and adult attempts at logic are unable to be heard. This is a common point of origin for behavioural outbursts. A strong sense of justice can be one of the greatest common themes, and justice-related cognitions such as 'it's not fair' should be explored robustly in relation to behavioural issues that are raised in sessions.

Many autistic children feel the weight of the world on their shoulders. They may feel the plight of refugees, war and climate change strongly. Sometimes this can lead to great despondence, fear and withdrawal. When social justice issues are uncovered and related cognitions explored, it can lead to momentous positive behaviour change involving hope and sometimes activism.

Family roles

It is common for ND children to feel worried about their place in the family, particularly those children who react with externalizing behaviours when overwhelmed. Due to the fact that they are often in trouble at home or at school, cognitions around their place in the family come into question. They can worry about being a burden to the family. It is also very common for ND children to develop beliefs that their neurotypical sibling is the 'easier' and therefore preferred child. Beliefs around the child's place within the family, particularly if siblings are involved, are often a necessary focus for cognitive work.

Self-concept

ND children can be particularly sensitive to comments from others. Well-meaning adults may tell them to pay no attention, but this can be enormously difficult. Children may fuse powerfully with comments others make, taking them as literal truths. Overhearing a peer say 'Dan is weird' can lead to Dan becoming strongly focused or hooked on the belief that he is weird for many years. Some have not been teased expressly, but judge themselves harshly after making a social faux pas. This can lead to beliefs such as 'I'm an idiot', 'I'm a loser' and 'nobody will ever forget this'. Comments from adults, especially those who are important to the young person, should also be considered. A flippant comment from a teacher, such as 'I'm disappointed you didn't finish the worksheet' might be taken on board powerfully by the child's mind, leading to beliefs about being hated by the teacher. The knock-on effect from a behavioural perspective can become very significant.

Depressive thoughts should also be considered. Some children hold beliefs about being a burden to their family and not deserving love or deserving to be punished. Thoughts common to ND young people at risk of depression may include the following:

Will anyone ever love me?

I'll never get a job.

My family would be better off without me.

Everyone already thinks I'm a loser; it's too late to make friends.

Executive functions

Executive function deficits are a key feature of ADHD and co-occur frequently with most forms of neurodiversity. The executive functions are a collection of processes that are responsible for guiding, directing and managing cognitive, emotional and behavioural functions. They include an ability to plan, organize, get started with work, stay on task and complete jobs on time. Western society highly values good executive functioning, so children and adults who are skilled in this area enjoy great advantages in terms of their ability to excel at school or at work. Intelligence is a separate construct to the executive functions. Many ND children are very bright but under-achieving at school because their executive functioning skills are poor and are interfering with their ability to complete tasks, leading to enormous frustration and giving up. Many ND children strongly value their intelligence and become unable to cope with the thought of needing extra help at school. This can lead to a worsening of grades and greater conflict at home.

When the executive function problem is explained to children compassionately, they are more likely to accept the type of help they might need.

Therapist: I want to chat to you about something we call executive functions. Execute means to make something happen. Let's imagine that your teacher asks you to do a creative writing piece. Now I know that you love creative writing; I've read some of the stuff you do in your spare time, so I know this is a task that could be great for you. I'd like to imagine a little cube in your brain that contains the idea for your creative writing piece for school. It's not in any order, but it is a mash-up of some incredibly wonderful ideas. In order for you to complete the task successfully, you need to find a way to get that cube out of your head and on to a piece of paper. This could take lots of steps, including remembering to do it in the first place, putting the ideas in order, finding paper or a laptop to write it on or handing it in on time. These steps help you to execute your story. They are your executive functions. You and I have talked about the fact that sometimes you struggle to get your ideas written down. I also know sometimes you leave things to the last minute. All of these troubles are about your executive functions. They have nothing to do with how clever you are!

Once the child has a clear understanding of the distinction between intelligence and executive functions, they are more likely to accept help with organization and planning. It will also help parents to advocate for an under-achieving child at school. For older children who have enjoyed learning about the brain in previous sessions, it can be useful to mention that the executive functions work out of the upstairs brain. As such, when anxiety is high, executive functions become poorer. Children can be guided to use anxiety reduction strategies to enhance their executive functioning.

Normalizing inner experiences

Once the child is more comfortable recognizing and discussing thoughts and feelings, many neurodivergent children will be better able to learn how their thoughts work generically. Some may express the following:

- They feel unable to stop the constant busy thoughts running through their minds.

- They hate their anxiety and experience troubles controlling it.

Interestingly, many young autistic people mistakenly believe that they have these unwanted inner experiences because they are autistic. They may not realize that these experiences are common to the human condition. This belief serves to enhance their struggle with their neurodivergence and their ability to manage difficulty when it shows up. It is therefore pertinent to provide appropriate psychoeducation around thoughts and feelings in the early stages of therapy as detailed throughout this book.

In the context of ND children, assisting them to make sense of these unpleasant inner sensations can be assisted by focusing on the following during discussion:

- All humans experience difficult feelings.

- Everyone experiences unwanted thoughts.

- All thoughts and feelings are normal.

- All thoughts and feelings pass.

Once the difficult thoughts and feelings have been identified, a therapist can readily implement strategies of cognitive defusion, self as context and acceptance as described in Chapter 8.

Bringing it all together

By this point, we have assisted the young person to develop skills in the following areas:

- Understanding my neurodivergent self.

- Recognizing my values.

- Understanding avoidance and struggle.

- Recognizing and managing difficult thoughts and feelings.

The groundwork is now set for moving in a valued direction. A young person's capacity to be willing to experience difficulty for the greater good can vary from day to day. The following script can be used as a template or modified to pull everything together. It is suggested that a whiteboard be used to create visuals analogous to the Away–Towards Line (Figure 10.1).

Figure 10.1

Amy

Amy decided she wanted to make some new friends but felt too shy to approach anyone. She loved art so her mum suggested she join the Tuesday Art Club at her school. This way, she could enjoy creating some art but would also have the chance to meet some other people with similar interests.

The next Tuesday lunchtime, Amy started moving TOWARDS the art class. As she approached the art room, she noticed her heart racing and a bunch of inside stuff got really busy. Her mind was telling her all sorts of things like 'they'll think I'm bad at art', 'they'll think I'm weird', 'I'm not really good at art anyway'. The worries got so loud that her mind then took a new path: 'there's probably nobody my age there anyway', 'I bet the art club isn't even on'. And with that, she turned AWAY and went back to reading her book on the bench. This made her feel much better. Her heart stopped racing, the unpleasant thoughts got quieter and she was able to enjoy her book in peace.

But the next day Amy started to worry again about having no friends. She decided to try art club the following Tuesday but the same thing happened. Only this time when she turned away from the art room, her fear of art club had somehow grown much bigger. This kept happening each week, until it felt impossible to try art club ever again.

Amy had learnt that moving AWAY from difficult inside stuff gave her relief pretty quickly. But she also discovered that it stopped her from getting what was truly important to her (making friends). The more AWAY moves she did, the harder it got to move TOWARDS what she really wanted.

If she truly wanted to make friends, she had to march through the hard stuff. There was no way around it. I'm not saying it's easy, but if Amy could have put one foot in front of the other and kept walking towards art club, even if her mind was telling her 'this is too hard', she might have had the chance for new friends. It wouldn't have been easy, but it would have been worth it.

Amy and many others have learned that we have to be willing to have some of that INSIDE DIFFICULT STUFF to achieve anything that is truly important to us.

- We can't get good grades without working hard.

- We can't have good friends without learning to handling disagreements.

- And we can't make new friends without risking rejection.

There's no way around it. We have to march through the difficulty.

The more we practise marching through difficulty and widening our comfort zone, the better we get at it. The first step is up to you – you just need to NOTICE when you are doing an AWAY or a TOWARDS move. Soon you'll get better at choosing towards moves and spending way more time doing the stuff that's important to you!

An extended version of this script is freely available on YouTube in child-friendly video form (Wassner 2021c).

Summary

Acceptance and Commitment Therapy is grounded in compassion, acceptance and an openness to difference. A therapist who lives these values will authentically express them in the therapy room, leading to warmth, understanding and fun. Neurodivergent children can be very sensitive to their surroundings and the language of those who speak to them. The acceptance canvas provides a wonderful start for building rapport thanks to its emphasis on social safety in the therapy room. When therapists provide a strengths-based approach to neurodiversity, the child's sense of social safety is enhanced. Therapists can build on this by recognizing and discussing key features of the autistic experience such as sensory processing, communication differences and common themes that contribute to anxiety and self-concept. ACT strategies that focus on noticing, accepting and defusing from difficult feelings and cognitions can then be discussed in a way that relates to ND learning preferences. In so doing, we are assisting neurodivergent children to spend more time engaging in a life that is meaningful and workable for them.

Chapter 11

An ACT Approach to Working with Parents

The ACT approach to parenting emphasizes compassionate acknowledgment of struggles experienced by both children and their parents. How parents approach their thoughts and feelings, particularly in the context of their relationship with their children, holds a valuable key to the pursuit of effective parenting. ACT principles can be utilized to assist parents in exploring their experiences and beliefs about their parenting and spending more time being the type of parent they truly want to be.

Children live within family systems, so working with children inevitably involves spending time with their parents. Families typically enter therapy when something is not working within the family system and the focus tends to be on what has gone wrong. To create a life that is more workable for families, it is important to gain an understanding of parents' expectations regarding themselves as parents, their children and the relationship between the two.

Parents tend to be very busy people. As they ferry their kids from school to activities and appointments, they may also be juggling careers, ageing parents and household tasks. A mindful approach to parenting encourages us to step out of the rat race, to pause and notice small moments in our daily lives. Unfortunately, many parenting moments are monopolized by routine matters such as brushing teeth and doing homework. There seems to be little time for pausing to smell the parenting roses. Within the safe context of a therapy room, where outside tasks are on pause, parents can be guided to mindfully consider what is truly important to them in the context of being a parent.

Values exploration

Experiential exercises can be utilized to commence the work of value discovery in parents. The following exercise offers a therapist three options for delivery based on their relationship with the parent and the parent's willingness to engage.

1. Presented as a worksheet.

2. Therapist collaborates with the parent via discussion.

3. A mindfulness exercise, guiding the parent to close their eyes and engage in deep breathing before thinking about the following questions.

Therapist: I'd like you to take a moment to think about yourself as a parent. If you could be the best version of a parent, what would that look like? What type of parent would you truly like to be? What would be your best parenting qualities?

Pause.

Now I'd like you to think about your child. Just bring your child to mind and picture them in this world. Think about what they do, where they play and how they learn. Imagine your child in different places: at home, at school, at a friend's house. Take a moment to think about your interactions with your child. Better moments, worse moments. And, finally, think about how you would truly like those interactions to be.

Based on this exercise, parents are invited to describe their parenting values. Common responses may include:

- patient

- understanding

- accepting

- approachable

- loving

- fun

- kind

- fair

- reliable.

The identified values should be written down and serve as a backdrop for ongoing discussions. The values list will become particularly important when helping parents to do hard stuff in the pursuit of a meaningful parent–child relationship.

First, however, we turn our attention to a parent's own responses to difficulty.

Role modelling acceptance of difficulty

ACT child therapists spend much of their time teaching children how to accept difficulty. Parents, too, must learn these skills in order to carry them over into real-life situations. Evolutionarily, parents are geared to comfort their distressed children. When a child is experiencing difficult feelings such as sadness or anxiety, parents often jump in quickly to 'fix' the problem. They might reassure their child and engage in behaviours that enable avoidance. For example, when a child feels too fearful to go somewhere new, such as playing at the home of a new friend, a parent might give in to the child and cancel the play date. In this way, the parent has enabled that very fear to perpetuate. As opposed to quickly rescuing one's child from distress, the ACT framework guides parents to acknowledge what is going on for their child and assist them in finding solutions. Before we can expect parents to encourage their children to face difficulty, parents first need to explore their own ability to navigate difficult thoughts and feelings.

The stress response is often a good place to start when it comes to helping parents recognize the function of their responses. Parents usually understand that their stress reactions can provide poor role modelling for children, but feel they lack the ability to manage themselves when high-stress situations emerge. Once a therapist has established adequate trust and rapport with a parent, they can explore the parent's own reaction to stress.

Therapist:

When you're really stressed at home with the kids, what do you do?

How about on a morning when you're rushing out the house and nobody's getting ready?

How do you handle frustrating phone calls to services, like when your internet needs fixing?

Do you ever have big reactions after chatting on the phone to someone in your family?

By letting the parent talk freely about their own reactions, we encourage the parent to think about how they usually handle stress. Most parents will tell you they realize they overreacted in certain situations. In high-stress situations, it can be hard to behave more calmly, even if we know that we do not want our kids to see us this way. Parents, however, can use these occasions to convey positive role modelling after the event. Assisting parents to debrief with children after these instances can help the young person learn about managing difficulty.

I know you heard me swear at the plumber yesterday. I'm quite embarrassed about that. It was really rude of me. He did do a rotten job on our toilet, but he didn't deserve to be yelled at by me. I'm going to apologize to him.

I think you overheard my chat with Aunty Trish yesterday. Neither of us behaved very well. Sometimes it's hard to hold in your anger when it's someone you love. I'm going to invite her and the kids over for tea tomorrow afternoon, so we can get back on track.

Parents can also choose moments to deliberately model positive coping. On the way to school, a parent might express:

Oh! I'm noticing my heart racing a bit. It makes me feel like I'm nervous or that maybe I forgot something. I'll take a few deep breaths at the next red light.

I'm not looking forward to work today. Lisa will be in the office, and she is always so loud and distracting. I'll just have to find a way to get on with my work while she bangs about in the next room.

In this way, children can learn to manage difficult feelings by noticing how their parent normalizes low-level difficulty.

Avoidance in parenting

In earlier chapters, a lot was said about how language affects what children believe and what they expect. Parent involvement during these child psychoeducation sessions, particularly those discussing the impact of avoidance and struggle, can be revisited with parents. In a brief review, parents are reminded that when inner difficulties emerge (thoughts, feelings, urges), our response to those difficulties is a crucial factor in determining the trajectory of those very difficulties. When we struggle or try too hard to rid ourselves of an uncomfortable feeling, it tends to grow bigger and more unmanageable. Avoidance of the struggle may provide relief in the short term but exacerbate the problem in the long term. A willingness to experience difficulty with an attitude of acceptance can be adopted in the pursuit of valued living.

Once it seems like the parent understands ACT's ideas about struggle and avoidance well, they are asked to think about their own patterns of avoidance.

Therapist: It's not easy being a parent. Sometimes it's all too hard, and we choose to avoid, even when we know it does not really help. Many of our avoidance strategies vary according to our mood or the situation. Let's start with those times when you just want to escape from it all. What are some of the avoidance strategies you use?

Common responses may include:

- alcohol

- binging on TV shows

- sex

- eating junk

- drugs

- going for a long run.

While debriefing these responses with the parent, a therapist should be careful to avoid giving judgement or advice about the noted avoidance actions; we merely observe that they are providing the function of avoidance. Some may be tempted to applaud going for a long run, but we must consider the intention behind the action. Going for a long run might appear healthy, but if the parent's intention when running was to get away from conflict at home, we consider it a form of avoidance. A parent can then be encouraged to reflect on the outcome of that avoidance, using similar questioning to that suggested for children in Chapter 1:

> How did that work out? Did it make the problem go away permanently?

> Did the problem keep coming back?

> Did it get you what you truly wanted?

This last question gives you a chance to talk about the parenting values you talked about earlier. Parents can be invited to provide their own example of a time they engaged in avoidance that was related to a parenting problem. This is followed up with the therapist questioning the workability of that response.

Case example: Sitting with discomfort around my own parenting

The following example relates to Deb, a mother of two children. She had been engaging in frequent conflict with her 9-year-old daughter, Sasha, usually about homework. When asked to provide an example of her own avoidance behaviour, Deb described the following:

> Last week I was helping Sasha with her history project. She had left it quite late, and there was still so much to do with only one day left until the project was due. I offered to help her, but all she cared about was making bright and colourful borders around her poster. I kept telling her we needed to get on to the writing, but she insisted on doing the pretty stuff first. We had been at it for over an hour with barely any progress. I had to cook dinner and had spent no time with Sasha's younger sister. I'm embarrassed to say I just lost it. I slammed the laptop shut as I told Sasha she needed to be better organized and not leave it to the last minute. Then I raised my voice and told her I wouldn't help her any further and that she deserved to fail the project.

Deb was able to recognize that her choice to stop assisting with the project was a form of avoidance. Deb had been sitting with her daughter for an hour, feeling frustrated and thinking about all of the other things she needed to be doing. Those were certainly uncomfortable thoughts and feelings. By leaving Sasha and her history project, Deb achieved two immediate gains: she could start cooking dinner and she was able to spend time with Sasha's sister. She would have also experienced avoidance-induced relief (reduced frustration) by moving away from the history project. Within a few minutes, however, the relief turned to stress on two separate accounts. First, the history project was not progressing. Second, Deb felt ashamed of her response to Sasha. During previous sessions Deb had identified two important parenting values: patience and reliability. Deb felt she had failed on both accounts. Deb also noticed that feelings of shame, guilt and embarrassment often showed up about Sasha and her homework. One could say that Deb had become fused with these beliefs about her parenting. Upon further discussion, Deb disclosed that Sasha had some learning difficulties and was particularly resistant when it came to writing tasks. Deb noted that she, herself, had struggled with writing tasks and felt guilty that Sasha had 'inherited her bad genes'. She added that although there was so much going on in the family, she wanted to prioritize her availability to assist Sasha with homework.

After figuring out some smaller logistical problems by enlisting help from others, Deb felt ready to deal with Sasha's homework. Deb would be guided to rethink her response with the hope of acting in a more values-based way in the future. We started with prediction: one could easily predict that there would be homework-related arguments in the future. By identifying a predictable scenario, such as homework completion, Deb could pre-empt the types of thoughts and feelings that would show up for her. Deb predicted the following:

Thoughts:

Here we go again… Why does she leave everything until the last minute?

Why can't she just get on with it?

I have things to do.

Feelings:

- tight chest

- headache

- clenched fists

- frustrated

- stressed.

Deb was then guided first to notice and then to make room for these thoughts and feelings in preparation for the next time the conflict would arise. The following exercise assists parents to explore their willingness to make room for difficulty in the service of valued living.

EXPERIENTIAL EXERCISE

Take a moment to close your eyes and settle into your chair. Take a few deep breaths at your own pace.

In a moment, I'd like you to start thinking about some of the difficulties you experience as a parent. What are the types of situations that can really feel tricky for you?

What are some of the things your mind tells you about the type of parent you are?

What are your expectations of yourself as a parent? Do you have lots of 'shoulds' about your parenting?

Pause.

And now I'd like you to think about the impact of having some of these beliefs about your parenting. Do these beliefs help you be the best parent you can be? Do they help you to be present with your kids? Is there something about these beliefs that pulls you away from your kids?

Pause.

Are you willing to make room for these difficult beliefs? Are you willing to sit with these difficult thoughts and still move in a valued direction as a parent?

Helpful thoughts

In addition to noticing and making room for difficult thoughts and sensations, parents can be assisted in planning some specific helpful cognitions. Parents can often predict the likely causes of conflict. This can be used to their advantage. In Deb's situation, her ability to predict future homework struggles will enable her to gain some distance (cognitive defusion) from the uncomfortable sensations. Helpful thoughts incorporating values can be built around these predictions to enhance Deb's chances of successfully engaging in acceptance of these difficult sensations:

> This is going to be frustrating, but I will continue sitting with Sasha because I want to model reliability and persistence.

> I can feel stressed and still provide her with my patience.

> I don't like the feeling of dinner being uncooked at 6 pm, but I'm willing to have dinner a little later on this occasion because Sasha has really struggled with school work and I want to show her I have confidence in her skills. It is not Sasha's fault that she struggles with writing.

Helpful thoughts can be written down to prepare Deb for the intense reactions she will likely experience the next time Sasha struggles with her homework. Deb can also be reminded to engage in some grounding exercises when the stress emerges, such as pausing and noticing her breath.

Parenting a dysregulated child
Reading a child's cues: Do they feel threatened or safe?
Many therapists working with children use the term 'dysregulated' to describe a state in which the young person's responses (behavioural and emotional) are poorly controlled. Unfortunately, many adults mistakenly perceive this behaviour as wilful or defiant. This type of adult reaction can exacerbate the situation, causing reactions on both sides to become bigger and trickier to manage. A dysregulated state of being is neither

pleasant nor deliberate for the child. In essence, a dysregulated child is probably feeling overwhelmed emotionally, leading to inappropriate behavioural or emotional responses.

When a child is dysregulated, their threat system has been activated. This results in greater rigidity and limits the child's ability to notice other points of view and self-regulate through the situation. When a parent recognizes that the child's poor self-control in this moment originates from a place of suffering and overwhelm, we invite more possibilities for managing the behaviour effectively and teaching the child important skills about self-regulation.

During moments of dysregulation, parents first need to assist the child to feel calmer or more regulated. The compassionate approach described for therapy in Chapter 2 can be applied by parents and comprises an essential feature of managing a dysregulated child. A parent who has participated in neuroscience psychoeducation, as described in Chapter 4, will be able to recognize that during moments of dysregulation the child is in fight-flight mode and therefore unable to access their upstairs brain or prefrontal cortex, impacting the child's ability to think clearly and make good decisions. Once this is recognized, the parent can make a more informed decision about how they will assist their child to better regulate. This is usually best achieved by the parent taking a calming stance and using language that helps the child feel heard. Often, repeating back the child's concerns can be a good start:

I can see that you really want your turn on the iPad.

Humans are designed to move towards attachment figures when they feel unsafe, so coaching the parent to be that safe harbour for the dysregulated child is paramount. Body language and tone may also assist the young person to co-regulate. Many children respond well to a calm, gentle tone of voice, crouching to the child's level and using gentle touch. This is not the case for all children, and therapists should spend time with parents to clarify this, ensuring that the parent can name what works to calm their individual child. Parents should also be invited to consider that certain calming strategies may be effective in some circumstances but not others. This can be managed by helping parents create calm, non-judgemental questions to ask their dysregulated child, including:

> I can see you're having a hard afternoon. Would you like some alone time, or would you like to sit here with me?

> You'd like alone time? No problem. I'll make sure nobody disturbs you, and if you need me, I'm just in the kitchen making myself a coffee.

Parents will be able to use this strategy most effectively when they are in tune with their child's mood and ability to regulate in any given moment. Often, parents have expectations and household rules which children are expected to follow. However, a child's capacity to fulfil these on any given day can fluctuate. This is true for even the most regulated children. Parents often say that they can predict their child's likely response when a demand is placed on them. Prediction is a fantastic tool that should be used to assist our parenting. If parents can see that their child is dysregulated after a hard day of school and can predict that they will melt down if asked to fold the laundry, then it may be best to drop that demand in that moment. After all, the meltdown can have a knock-on effect for the rest of the family and the rest of the day. The skills and home values that children can acquire by folding laundry may be better learned at another time.

Imagine, in a particular family there is a rule that when you come home from school, you take your lunchbox out of your bag and place it in the sink. In this example, a child is in the back seat of their parent's car after school. The parent can clearly see that the child has had a hard day even though no words have been spoken. Upon entering the house, the parent could choose to insist on putting the lunchbox in the sink. It's only a small task and, of course, it is a family rule. However, the parent might consider using their child's unhappy demeanour as an opportunity to build connection:

> Riley, I can see you've had a hard day. I'll put your lunchbox in the sink today. Let me know if you need anything.

Although Riley has said nothing about his problems, he feels heard and seen by his parent. He is also more likely to open up to his parent that afternoon, building further connection and potentially having the chance to problem-solve together.

Some parents worry that by dropping household expectations every time their child is dysregulated, nothing will ever get done. Indeed, in the early stages of this technique, that may be the case. But as time passes and connections develop, expectations can be increased.

A child's history of feeling heard and seen by their parent can have an ongoing impact on the child's threat system and ability to navigate problematic situations. Within a family system, social safety is important, so a parent acknowledging their child's point of view, particularly when the conflict involves a sibling, can assist the child in being less reactive. By experiencing a sense of safety in such circumstances, neuronal connections are being made, strengthening the child's ability to feel safe in this moment and over time. The more times this happens, the more brain connections are made in this direction, leading to a better long-term prognosis for self-regulation capacity (Siegel and Bryson 2012). A parent who consistently helps their child feel seen, heard and soothed is achieving two important goals:

- prevention and management of meltdowns in the short term

- investment in the child's long-term capacity to self-regulate.

Case example: Choosing when to drop demands

Jared was a friendly 7-year-old boy who had been coming home from school more dysregulated than usual. One afternoon, he was teasing his brother in the car and answering his mother's questions in a snappy tone. When they arrived home, Kim, Jared's mother, asked him to tidy his room before watching television. Jared threw down his bag and started kicking the wall. In the past, Kim would have become firmer, raised her voice and banned screens for the rest of the week. After some parent coaching sessions, she was able to step back and notice what was happening. In particular, she recognized that this behaviour was unlike Jared and something was clearly not right. She chose to drop the expectation about tidying the room and prioritize connection by saying the following:

> Hey, Jared, I can see something's wrong. It's not like you to kick the wall. It's okay, we can tidy your room later. Come and sit down with me.

On this occasion, Jared was able to stop kicking the wall. He sat on the couch with his arms folded, briefly mumbling about how unfair chores are. Kim knew that chores were never a true problem in their home and recognized that there was more to the story. She guessed that complaining about chores was simply a plausible thing for Jared to say in the moment. Calmly, she acknowledged his concerns:

> I didn't realize that was bothering you but I think you know kicking the wall won't help. I'm happy to come up with a new plan about when you tidy your room. We can chat about that later. For now, I can see you've had a rough day. How about I make you a hot chocolate and you can play with Comet (dog)?

Some parents might be concerned that this response is overly permissive and rewards inappropriate behaviour. Of course, each situation needs to be considered individually but, in this instance, Kim recognized that Jared was experiencing difficulties somewhere else. Once Jared had calmed down, Kim joined him and gently probed around the edges of the social situation:

> I've noticed you don't talk about Matt anymore. Is everything okay between you two?

Jared was calm enough to discuss what was happening at school. Although Matt wasn't the issue, other boys were, and Kim's compassionate and open approach provided an opportunity for Jared to open up. Kim assisted him to explore what was going wrong at school and helped him to navigate some stressful situations. Afterwards, they tidied his room together.

The benefits of this approach are many. First, Kim and Jared's relationship is strengthened. Jared feels heard and recognizes that he can approach his mother with future problems. This could be further reinforced if they are lucky enough to have yielded some good results on the playground. Jared is also learning the skills of regulation, hopefully enhancing his ability to problem-solve effectively in the future. It is also likely that Jared and Kim are now in a better position to work out long-term agreements about room tidying.

Case example: Prioritizing connection

Bryce was a bright 9-year-old boy who usually excels in English and has never struggled to complete his work. One Tuesday afternoon, he came home in an irritable mood. His mother guided him to commence his English homework, and within two minutes, he started to say, 'I can't do it.'

His mother knew that Bryce could complete the work with ease and exclaimed, 'You've done way harder stuff than this. Come on, you've got this.' Although his mother intended to be encouraging, Bryce's mind was already in threat mode, and he viewed her words as dismissive. Bryce's mother was appealing to the sensible part of his brain that recognized the ease of the task. Unfortunately, Bryce had limited access to this part of the brain as he was firmly entrenched in the downstairs brain. Bryce felt he was neither believed nor heard, and his frustration built. He exclaimed, 'I'm dumb', 'this is too hard' and 'the teacher hates me'.

Once his mother recognized that Bryce's mind was in threat mode, she recalled the importance of helping Bryce feel heard and gently said the following:

> You really wanted to be able to answer that question, but it was very hard. I know you care deeply about your school work. It must be so frustrating when you don't understand the question.

From here, Bryce felt heard and safe. This enabled him to accept help from his mother and slowly face the task at hand.

Staying calm in the face of chaos

There are times when the child's point of view is completely nonsensical. It can be truly testing for parents to provide unconditional compassion and empathy, particularly if the child's behaviour is highly inappropriate, or when their arguments are illogical. It can also be hard for parents to resist the temptation to logically argue the facts. Parents can be reminded to keep in mind the fact that their child is struggling to handle something difficult and has likely lost access to their sensible thinking. A well-evidenced argument from the parent is unlikely to be comprehended by the child and certainly not likely to help the young person calm down. When a child is dysregulated, the parent's job is to remain calm. A reactive parent only adds to the dysregulation, and the situation can deteriorate quickly.

It must be acknowledged that in these moments parents are usually tired and overwhelmed. Asking parents to remain calm can be very delicate, particularly if these events are occurring frequently. As much as we need to acknowledge that parents need to 'release' their stress too, from a child–parent conflict perspective there is nothing to be gained from adding a parent's dysregulation to a volatile situation. Sometimes parents need to be very good actors and hold it together until the storm has passed. It is indeed a big ask. Parents in these situations should be encouraged to prioritize self-care at other times, including accessing individual therapy to assist them in processing and managing their reactions to such situations. Until then, acceptance strategies can be tweaked to assist parents in better self-regulating through their child's outbursts.

Acceptance of a child's intense dysregulation

There are times when a child's dysregulated behaviour is more extreme. Many refer to these situations as meltdowns. Meltdowns are undeniably unpleasant experiences for the child and for the parent. When a child is in this state, they are far from happy. They are feeling overwhelmed and out of control. Parents, too, are usually overwhelmed.

An ACT perspective would encourage parents to treat the meltdown as a deeply unpleasant experience that we need to learn to live with. In the context of acceptance, we would be treating the meltdown as our sparring partner. In this way, we are learning to live with the meltdown rather than having it rule our lives.

When a parent is able to view a meltdown as a cry for help from a child who is very dysregulated, we are beginning the work of acceptance. Parents can be encouraged to view the behaviour as 'connection seeking' rather than 'attention seeking'. This gives the parent an opening into the space they need to remain composed. In order to maintain calm, parents will require further cognitive skills. As acceptance involves a willingness to experience difficulty, we want to deter parents from clenching their teeth as they wait for the meltdown to pass. Rather, we can teach parents the skills of accepting and moving through the meltdown, even though it is unpleasant.

Therapist to parent: I'm sorry to hear the meltdowns have been increasing. You must be so exhausted. How have you been doing with trying to stay calm and letting him know you understand what he is upset about?

We've talked about recognizing the meltdown as a cry for help rather than wilful defiance. Does bringing that to mind help you to help him?

From here we can increase skill building by incorporating a link to the parent's identified parenting values.

Therapist: I recognize that asking you to stay calm has been really taxing on you. I'd like to try something new today to assist you in moving through the meltdowns with better focus and meaning. Are you, as a parent, willing to navigate this meltdown in a way that may feel difficult for you but could help your child in the long term? Is there any way you could view the next meltdown as an opportunity to help your child feel safe and loved?

We've talked a lot about brain connections. So, next time this happens, you could remind yourself that if your child can move through a meltdown in a way that involves you demonstrating patience, safety and love, we will be assisting them to self-regulate and self-soothe. Over time, they will improve in these skills and eventually be better able to develop other skills such as independence and resilience.

The following helpful thoughts (self-talk cognitions) incorporating acceptance, compassion and a link to values can be introduced to parents to reinforce their capacity to move through the meltdown.

This is really unpleasant, but I'm going to stay calm and show my child I am there for them.

I'm feeling scared inside, but I am showing my child that I am a safe place for them. That way, they will be given the best opportunity to learn self-regulation.

I just want to get out of here, but I will stay present for my child because I want them to grow up to be resilient and independent.

I could just walk out of the house right now and avoid all of this stress, or I can be present with them until they are able to calm themselves down.

I'm not going back on my screen-time promise, and I know they won't like that. I'm willing to let them scream this out because it will help them learn the skills they need for friendships.

Post-meltdown: A wonderful parenting opportunity
Once the incident has passed and the child has been able to calm down,

parents are encouraged to debrief with their child. This moment is an opportunity to reinforce connection and safety. For some, apologies and forgiveness can be managed in this moment. For others, it might just be a continuation of the parent's body language and tone communicating safety.

Is there something I could do differently next time that would help you handle it better?

On some occasions, it is necessary to discuss consequences. If the child has deliberately hurt someone or something, repairs need to be considered. This should only be explored once the child has regained access to their prefrontal cortex (upstairs brain). In this way, the child can be held accountable but within a context of safety, reconnection and understanding. It is usually best to choose a repair method that is related to the damage.

Let's get some tape and repair the book. Here, I'll help you...

Some children will feel able to apologize for their behaviour whereas others will not. This is an important life skill, but if your child is not ready, a parent can role model an apology:

I'm sorry I yelled at you. I wish I could have handled it differently.

In this way, the parent is not getting caught up in the content of the argument (right versus wrong), but rather taking responsibility for their behaviour during the argument.

Summary

The ACT approach to parenting acknowledges the difficulties and struggles experienced by both children and their parents. Effective parent coaching considers how parents approach their thoughts and feelings, particularly in the context of their relationship with their children. Parents can be guided to spend more time being the type of parent they truly want to be by exploring parenting values and committing to engaging in action that is consistent with those values, even when conflict and stress emerge within the family system.

References

American Psychiatric Association (2013). *Diagnostic and Statistical Manual of Mental Disorders* (5th edn). Washington, DC: Jaypee Brothers Medical Publishers.

Fredrickson, B. L. and Joiner, T. (2002). Positive emotions trigger upward spirals toward emotional well-being. *Psychological Science 13*, 2, 172–5.

Gilbert, P. A. (2009). *The Compassionate Mind: A New Approach to Life Challenges*. London: Constable and Robinson.

Harris, R. H. (2009). *ACT Made Simple*. Oakland, CA: New Harbinger.

Harry Potter and the Philosopher's Stone (2001). Directed by Chris Columbus. Feature film. CA: Warner Bros.

Hayes, S. C., Strosahl, K. D. and Wilson, K. G. (1999). *Acceptance and Commitment Therapy: An Experiential Approach to Behavior Change*. New York: Guilford.

Hours, C., Recasens, C. and Baleyte, J. (2022). ASD and ADHD comorbidity: What are we talking about? *Frontiers in Psychiatry 13*, 837424.

Porges, S. W. (2009). The polyvagal theory: New insights into adaptive reactions of the autonomic nervous system. *Cleveland Clinic Journal of Medicine 76 (Suppl 2)*, S86–S90.

Rowling, J. K. (1999). *Harry Potter and the Goblet of Fire*. New York: Bloomsbury.

Samantaray, N. N., Chaudhury, S. and Singh, P. (2018). Efficacy of inhibitory learning theory-based exposure and response prevention and selective serotonin reuptake inhibitor in obsessive-compulsive disorder management: A treatment comparison. *Industrial Psychiatry Journal 27*, 1, 53–60.

Schreiner, I. and Malcolm, J. (2008). The benefits of mindfulness meditation: Changes in emotional states of depression, anxiety, and stress. *Behaviour Change 25*, 3, 156–68.

Siegel, D. J. and Bryson, T. P. (2012). *The Whole-Brain Child: 12 Revolutionary Strategies to Nurture Your Child's Developing Mind*. New York: Random House.

Singer, J. (2017). *Neurodiversity: The Birth of an Idea*. Amazon Kindle eBook, self-published.

The Wizard of Oz (1939). Directed by Victor Fleming. Feature film. CA: Metro-Goldwyn-Mayer.

Tirch, D., Schoendorff, B. and Silberstein, L. R. (2014). *The ACT Practitioner's Guide to the Science of Compassion: Tools for Fostering Psychological Flexibility*. Oakland, CA: New Harbinger.

Wassner, J. (2021a, Sept 15). *Fight Flight for Kids*. Curious Kids Psychology, YouTube Video. www.youtube.com/watch?v=1VQUOr-R3eA.

Wassner, J. (2021b, Sept 15). *Brain Science for Kids – Thinking and Feeling*. Curious Kids Psychology, YouTube Video. www.youtube.com/watch?v=6Rn386arno8.

Wassner, J. (2021c, Sept 25). *Avoiding It vs Facing It.* Curious Kids Psychology, YouTube Video. www.youtube.com/watch?v=jWnGW3ezs7k.

Wassner, J. (2021d, Sept 30). *Torch on the Brain.* Curious Kids Psychology, YouTube Video. www.youtube.com/watch?v=sV9uYKdIUXg.

Wassner, J. and Fleming, G. (2015). *Mindtrain: A Treatment Manual for Psychologists Working with Anxious Children in the Spirit of Acceptance and Commitment Therapy.* https://pdfcoffee.com/mindtrain-manualpdf-pdf-free.html.

Waters, L., Cameron, K., Nelson-Coffey, D., Crone, M. *et al.* (2021). Collective well-being and posttraumatic growth during COVID-19: How positive psychology can help families, schools, workplaces and marginalized communities. *The Journal of Positive Psychology 17*, 6, 761–89.

Yildiz, M. and Eldeleklioqlu, J. (2021). The relationship between decision-making and intolerance to uncertainty, cognitive flexibility and happiness. *Eurasian Journal of Educational Research 91*, 39–60.

Further Reading

APA Presidential Task Force on Evidence-Based Practice (2006). Evidence-based practice in psychology. *American Psychologist 61,* 271–85.

Biglan, A. (2015). *The Nurture Effect: How the Science of Human Behavior Can Improve Our Lives and Our World.* Oakland, CA: New Harbinger.

Boone, M. S. and Canicci, J. (2013). Acceptance and commitment therapy in groups. In J. Pistorello (ed.) *Mindfulness and Acceptance for Counseling College Students.* Oakland, CA: New Harbinger.

Clarke, S., Kingston, J., James, Bolderston, H. and Remington, B. (2014). Acceptance and commitment therapy group for treatment-resistant participants: A randomized control trial. *Journal of Contextual Behavioral Science 3,* 179–88.

Coyne, L. W. and Murrell, A. R. (2009). *The Joy of Parenting: An Acceptance and Commitment Therapy Guide to Effective Parenting in the Early Years.* Oakland, CA: New Harbinger.

Dixon, M. (2016, June). Using RFT and ACT to optimize therapy for individuals with autism. ACBS International. Workshop conducted from Association for Contextual Behavioral Science, Seattle, WA.

Dixon, M. (2014). *Acceptance and Commitment Therapy for Children with Autism and Emotional Challenges.* Carbondale, IL: Shawnee Scientific Press.

Hayes, S. C. (2004). Acceptance and commitment therapy, relational frame theory, and the third wave of behavioral and cognitive therapies. *Behavior Therapy 35,* 639–65.

Hayes, S. C., Luoma, J., Bond, F., Masuda, A. and Lillis, J. (2006). Acceptance and Commitment Therapy: Model, processes, and outcomes. *Behaviour Research and Therapy 44, 1,* 1–25.

Hayes, S. C., Strosahl, K. and Wilson, K. (1999). *Acceptance and Commitment Therapy: An Experiential Approach to Behavior Change.* New York: Guilford.

Luoma, J. B., Hayes, S. C. and Walser, R. D. (2007). *Learning ACT.* Oakland, CA: New Harbinger.

McCurry, C. (2009). *Parenting Your Anxious Child with Mindfulness and Acceptance: A Powerful New Approach to Overcoming Fear, Panic and Worry Using Acceptance and Commitment Therapy.* Oakland, CA: New Harbinger.

Ramnero, J. and Torneke, T. (2011). *The ABCs of Human Behavior: Behavioral Principles for the Practicing Clinician.* Oakland, CA: New Harbinger.

Siegel, D. J. and Hartzell, M. (2003). *Parenting from the Inside Out.* New York: Penguin.

Deborah Schroder

BUILDING
BETTER
THERAPEUTIC
RELATIONSHIPS
WITH CHILDREN

A Creative Activity Workbook

Building Better Therapeutic Relationships with Children

A Creative Activity Workbook

Deborah Schroder

£22.99 | $32.95 | PB | 96PP |
ISBN 978 1 78775 968 8 |
eISBN 978 1 78775 969 5

Learn how to start, develop and sustain strong therapeutic relationships with children by rediscovering your inner child with this easy-to-use workbook, filled with ideas, activities and reusable Q&A worksheets.

Focusing on creating a partnership in the therapy room, chapters include hands-on guidance on how building relationships with children can differ to adult relationship building, adapting activities to a variety of settings and starting the relationship. Work through the chapters to resolve challenges in the therapeutic relationship often faced by those working with children and families, such as anger, anxiety, reticence, problems with separation and change, and saying goodbye.

Introducing creativity into the work, these exercises will integrate seamlessly into your practice every day.

Deborah Schroder is a therapist and best-selling art therapy author. She was the chairperson of the Art Therapy/Counseling Program at Southwestern College, where she also created the Children's Mental Health Certificate Program. She has served on the New Mexico Counseling and Therapy Practice licensing board and on the board for CASA First. Deborah currently provides clinical supervision at the Eight Northern Pueblos.

Conversation-Starters for Working with Children and Adolescents After Trauma

Simple Cognitive and Arts-Based Activities

Dawn D'Amico, LCSW, PhD

£17.99 | $24.95 | PB | 224PP | ISBN 978 1 78775 144 6 | eISBN 978 1 78775 145 3

It can be challenging for children and adolescents who have experienced trauma to feel safe and confident enough to talk. Conversation-Starters for Working with Children and Adolescents After Trauma aims to make this process easier for practitioners by offering gentle, playful techniques to help children to start to open up.

With over 80 activities tailored to different styles of communication, all requiring minimal preparation, this flexible resource provides an activity for every situation: from helping a child identify fun things around them and recognize feelings, to enabling them to learn how to control unwanted thoughts. Organized into Coping and Positive Thinking activities, each of the ideas can be used in both individual and group formats, and case studies throughout the book serve as helpful guides on how they work in practice.

A brilliant source of easy-to-implement ideas and techniques for use with children aged 5+ and adolescents, it will be valued by those supporting children who have experienced trauma or abuse, as well as those working with children with mental health challenges.

Dawn D'Amico, LCSW, PhD, is a psychotherapist who has 26 years of experience working with children affected by various types of trauma in different settings, including private practice, hospitals, children's homes, and refugee camps. She has worked internationally in Asia, Africa, Australia, and Canada, and has served as a graduate faculty member at the University of Wisconsin. She lives in Wisconsin, USA.

Superhero Therapy for Anxiety and Trauma

A Professional Guide with ACT and CBT-based Activities and Worksheets for All Ages

Janina Scarlet

Illustrated by Dean Rankine
Foreword by Dennis Tirch

£22.99 | $32.95 | PB | 224PP |
ISBN 978 1 78775 554 3 |
eISBN 978 1 78775 555 0

Drawing on ACT and CBT, this book incorporates popular culture into evidence-based therapy, offering a unique approach to supporting clients with anxiety and trauma. With activities and downloadable worksheets, it is a complete guide to the popular Superhero Therapy approach. The approach encourages clients to identify with superheroes and other pop culture characters, learn superhero powers, face their fears, and reframe experiences as their origin story in their superhero journey.

The approach helps to validate clients' experiences, alleviating shame and stigma surrounding mental health, and encourages deeper understanding and reflection during sessions. It can be used in a variety of settings with children aged 7+, teens, and adults.

Janina Scarlet is a clinical psychologist and Lead Trauma Specialist at the Center for Stress and Anxiety Management in San Diego. She is the developer of Superhero Therapy and has been awarded the United Nations Association Eleanor Roosevelt Human Rights Award for her work on the approach.

Dean Rankine is a Ledger- and Stanley Award-winning comic book artist and illustrator best known for his work on *Simpsons Comics*. His other credits include *Futurama, Rick and Morty, Invader Zim, Underdog, Hellboy,* and *Oggy and the Cockroaches.*

CREATIVE WAYS
TO HELP CHILDREN
MANAGE ANXIETY
IDEAS AND ACTIVITIES FOR WORKING
THERAPEUTICALLY WITH WORRIED
CHILDREN AND THEIR FAMILIES

DR FIONA ZANDT AND
DR SUZANNE BARRETT
FOREWORD BY DR KAREN CASSIDAY

Creative Ways to Help Children Manage Anxiety

Ideas and Activities for Working Therapeutically with Worried Children and Their Families

Dr Fiona Zandt and Dr Suzanne Barrett

Illustrated by Richy K. Chandler

Foreword by Dr Karen Cassiday

£24.99 | $35.00 | PB | 208PP | ISBN 978 1 78775 094 4 | eISBN 978 1 78775 095 1

This book sets out therapeutic activities to help children aged 4–12 and their families to better understand and manage anxiety. It explains how to work with anxious children, providing a framework that draws on CBT, ACT, and narrative therapy approaches. Practical tips for therapists are included and important developmental considerations are discussed, including adapting therapy for children with developmental difficulties, and working with families and schools.

Over 50 playful therapeutic activities are included, giving children an arsenal of coping strategies. They focus on key areas such as understanding anxiety, managing anxious thoughts, and building resilience, and use readily available, inexpensive materials and downloadable templates which are provided in the book. This is the perfect tool for therapists looking for ways to work with children with anxiety.

Dr Fiona Zandt and **Dr Suzanne Barrett** are clinical psychologists who each have over 18 years' experience working therapeutically with children and families in a broad range of settings. They founded Creative Child Therapy Workshops in 2014 (www.childpsychologyworkshops.com.au), providing in-person and online workshops for therapists, and have previously written *Creative Ways to Help Children Manage BIG Feelings*.